Perennials
FOR
DUMMIES®
PORTABLE EDITION

by Marcia Tatroe
& the Editors of The National
Gardening Association

WILEY

Wiley Publishing, Inc.

Perennials For Dummies, Portable Edition

Published by
Wiley Publishing, Inc.
111 River St.
Hoboken, NJ 07030-5774
www.wiley.com

WILEY

About the Authors

Marcia Tatroe is a garden designer, lecturer, and writer who lives on the southeastern edge of Denver, Colorado. She settled on a career in gardening after studying art and interior design in Southern California, raising kids, and actively wondering what she would be when she grew up. In the meantime, she was fortunate to have the opportunity to live and garden in areas as diverse as Highland, California; Tacoma, Washington; Lompoc, California; the Netherlands; and south-central England. When she discovered folks would actually pay to hear her gush on about gardening, there was no looking back.

A former Master Gardener of several years for Colorado State University's Cooperative Extension Program, Marcia is currently on the board of directors of Xeriscape Colorado! and a teacher for Denver Botanic Gardens. An inveterate plant addict, she squeezes an ever-changing collection of over 2,000 perennials into a small suburban lot. Time spent tending the garden is one of her greatest passions, and she hopes it's contagious.

The National Gardening Association is the largest member-based, nonprofit organization of home gardeners in the U.S. Founded in 1972 (as Gardens for All) to spearhead the community-garden movement, today's National Gardening Association is best known for its bimonthly magazine, *National Gardening*. Some half-million gardeners worldwide read each issue of this publication, which reports on all aspects of home gardening. The National Gardening Association supplements these publishing activities with online efforts at www.garden.org.

Dedication

To my patient husband, Randy Tatroe, who typed this whole darn book from my unintelligible scribblings (and with only a reasonable amount of grumbling).

Publisher's Acknowledgments

We're proud of this book; please send us your comments through our Dummies online registration form located at www.dummies.com/register/.

Some of the people who helped bring this book to market include the following:

Acquisitions, Editorial, and Media Development

Project Editor: Laura Peterson Nussbaum

Acquisitions Editor: Kristin A. Cocks

Editorial Program Coordinator: Hanna K. Scott

Technical Editor: The National Gardening Association

Editorial Manager: Michelle Hacker

Editorial Supervisor and Reprint Editor: Carmen Krikorian

Editorial Assistants: Erin Calligan, David Lutton

Cover Photo: Dynamic Graphics

Illustrations: Ron Hildebrand, Hildebrand Design

Cartoons: Rich Tennant (www.the5thwave.com)

Composition Services

Project Coordinator: Kristie Rees

Layout and Graphics: Carl Byers, Joyce Haughey, Kathie Rickard

Proofreaders: Leeann Harney, Jessica Kramer

Indexer: Sherry Massey

Publishing and Editorial for Consumer Dummies

Diane Graves Steele, Vice President and Publisher, Consumer Dummies

Joyce Pepple, Acquisitions Director, Consumer Dummies

Kristin A. Cocks, Product Development Director, Consumer Dummies

Michael Spring, Vice President and Publisher, Travel

Kelly Regan, Editorial Director, Travel

Publishing for Technology Dummies

Andy Cummings, Vice President and Publisher, Dummies Technology/General User

Composition Services

Gerry Fahey, Vice President of Production Services

Debbie Stailey, Director of Composition Services

Contents at a Glance

Table of Contents

Introduction

*I*f your only experience with gardening until now has been tending houseplants, you're in for a real treat when you turn your hand to perennial gardening. Anyone can grow perennials; houseplants are the ones that give gardening a bad name. I'll let you in on a secret — I couldn't keep a houseplant healthy if my life depended on it. (When I entertain guests, I run out and buy robust replacements so that I'm not embarrassed by the dead and dying plants hanging around from the last party.) But I can grow hundreds of perennials. Most perennials are much less demanding and tolerate much more abuse than you may have been led to believe.

The only trick to creating a little bit of heaven in your own yard is choosing perennials suited to the conditions where you live. Every corner of the world has flowers that grow better there than anywhere else on earth. Every location also has flowers that don't survive there no matter what you do. Concentrate on the flowers in the first group, instead of pining for the flowers in the second group, and you absolutely can't fail.

Like all nonessential activities in life, gardening, first and foremost, ought to be fun. Don't get bogged down in shoulds and should nots — just go with your own instincts. If you aren't having a good time, you're either trying too hard or attempting to live up to someone else's expectations.

About This Book

This book is just to get you started; the best lessons come by trial and error in your own garden. Every gardener's experience is unique, so treat all gardening advice — including mine — with a healthy dose of skepticism. Be especially skeptical whenever what you read contradicts your own garden. Your garden tells you what it likes and doesn't like.

How to Use This Book

You don't need to read this book from cover to cover — it's not a romance novel or a who-done-it thriller, for heaven's sake. Instead, let it serve as a reference you can turn to whenever a particular need arises. Use the Table of Contents or the Index to guide you to the section you need, or simply skim through chapters or parts of the book that look relevant to you.

Before you actually put your shovel to the ground, be sure to give some attention to the fundamentals of selection, care, and feeding. These basics, covered in the following chapters, are all interrelated — overlooking any one of them can be fatal (for your perennials, that is):

- Chapters 2 and 3: Choosing perennials compatible with your climate
- Chapter 6: Soil preparation
- Chapter 7: How to plant
- Chapter 8: Watering
- Chapter 9: Fertilizing
- Chapter 10: Taking care of the garden

Icons Used in This Book

Gardening is a visual art, so using icons to depict certain kinds of information is only natural in a gardening book. When you see the following icons beside a paragraph, here's what you can expect to find:

A big part of gardening involves keeping the grim reaper out of the flower bed. Flower Killer icons can help by calling your attention to any practices or products that can suck the life out of your prized perennials.

Sometimes, it seems as though gardeners speak a language all their own. In this book, I try to avoid all that botanical mumbo-jumbo. But some gardening terms are worth learning, if for nothing else than to get the sales clerk at the local nursery to understand what you want. Whenever you see the Garden Jargon icon, limber up your tongue and prepare for a lesson in Gardenese.

 Which plants grow well for you and which ones die the moment their roots hit the soil depends on your climate, soil type, and many other factors unique to your garden. However, some perennials seem to have the fortitude of a Saturday morning cartoon hero, no matter where they're planted. I indicate these rough-and-tumble plants with the Perennial Superhero icon.

 In the midst of digging, weeding, watering, pinching, pruning, and planting, you can easily lose sight of the big picture. Remember icons adorn paragraphs that help you put everything in perspective. (For added effect, you may want to read these pearls of wisdom in your mother's voice.)

 Gardening should be fun, so don't let yourself get caught up in a sticky situation. Thorny Issue icons serve as beacons to steer you clear of common gardening blunders that can cause you to lose time, money, and patience.

 A favorite pastime of gardeners is sharing trade secrets with other gardeners. Look for the Tip icon to find helpful hints that can make you the most popular gardener on the block.

 Although gardening is a relatively safe hobby, you do need to be aware of some potential health and safety hazards. Some plants and plant-care products are deadly poisonous. Treat paragraphs with the Warning icon the same way you treat warning labels on household chemicals: Read them carefully and heed their advice.

Where to Go from Here

Be honest. You've probably already read the chapters that first caught your fancy. Few folks ever tackle the Introduction first. If you are the rare exception, stop reading this introduction right now. Instead, thumb through the pages and read the bits that interest you most. That will be enough of an orientation to what this book covers.

"That should do it."

Chapter 1

Perennials: The Plant That Keeps On Going

*P*erennial flowers are in the midst of a popularity surge. Actually, perennials never lost their appeal in gardening circles, but when perennial gardens start popping up in the landscapes of every new gas station or shopping mall, you can't help but notice that a mainstream insurgence is afoot.

Nurseries can hardly keep up with the demand as the public clamors for more varieties. (After they've gotten a taste of the mundane, gardeners start craving the new and the rare.) Fund-raising garden tours sell out. Plant clubs and societies find their membership rolls swelling. Subscription rates of gardening magazines soar.

With this book, you can discover for yourself what all the fuss is about. You don't need to hire a professional gardener to surround your home with perennials — you can grow them yourself. Perennials are as easy to grow as they are fulfilling.

What Makes a Perennial a Perennial?

Rather than bury you here in Chapter 1 under dozens of terms concerning every facet of perennial gardening, I've decided to define most terms as they come up in the appropriate chapters. This chapter includes only a few of the most basic definitions to help you make sense of the topic at large. (Relax, there isn't a quiz at the end of this chapter.)

The many meanings of "perennial"

A perennial is any plant that lives for three or more years when it's grown in conditions to its liking. Notice that just because a plant dies in less than three years doesn't mean that it isn't a perennial (otherwise, I know several people who would claim that there's no such thing as a perennial — at least not in their yards). The fact that you can't get Mexican sage to last a week in your Alaskan flowerbed doesn't mean that Mexican sage isn't a perennial. Like all perennials, Mexican sage has the potential to live a long and full life, if you grow it in the proper conditions.

This book is really just about one type of perennial plant — the *herbaceous flowering perennial*. Technically, the term "perennial" includes such giants as the majestic, centuries-old redwood and the oak tree in the city park. Unlike trees and shrubs (which have woody stems forming their twigs, branches, and trunks) herbaceous perennials have soft, fleshy stems.

Perennials that hail from cold climates usually indulge in a winter nap, called a period of *dormancy*. (A few herbaceous perennials go dormant in summer, instead, playing a convincing game of opossum for their uninitiated gardeners.) During the period of dormancy, the perennial dies back to the ground — that is, allows its stems and foliage to die. The aboveground parts of a dormant plant are truly dead, but the roots are alive and well. In fact, the roots may be actively growing even when the top is resting.

In more moderate climates, most herbaceous perennials are *evergreen* (meaning that their aboveground parts are alive and kicking all year long) because they don't need a coping mechanism such as dormancy to escape extreme temperatures.

Anatomy of a perennial

Growing perennials is much easier if you have at least a fundamental understanding of how the flowers are put together. Significant variations exist within this large group of plants, but they all share a few characteristics, as shown in Figure 1-1.

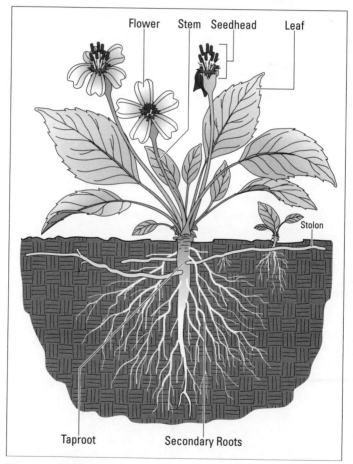

Figure 1-1: The basic parts of a perennial plant are the roots, stem, leaves, flowers, and seedheads.

Roots

In addition to serving as the anchor that holds the perennial in place, roots also pull water and nutrients from the soil and carry these essentials to the stems. The roots even store extra water and nutrients in case times get tough.

The two main types of roots are fibrous roots and taproots. Fibrous-rooted perennials have a network of branching roots. Taprooted perennials have a fleshy central root (like a carrot), with smaller secondary roots growing off the main root (refer to Figure 1-1). Whereas taproots can reach quite deeply into the ground, fibrous roots generally occur primarily in the top 12 inches (30 cm) of soil.

Stems

Stems are the framework of the perennial, supporting the leaves and flowers. They also transport water and nutrients from the roots to the leaves and flowers, and vice versa. Stems take many forms. Some are squared, and some are rounded. They may be upright or low and spreading; single or branched.

Stem tissue is sometimes specialized to create thickened underground repositories, where the plant can stash extra food and water. These lumps of tissue take many forms, such as *rhizomes, corms,* or *tubers.*

Perennials may also spread by modified stems called *stolons* (or runners) that travel just beneath the surface of the ground (refer to Figure 1-1). The stolons often send up new shoots along their length, either close by or quite some distance from the original clump, depending on the perennial. Some perennials can make pests of themselves — their runners spreading far too quickly. But these plants can also provide you with lots of new plants.

Leaves

Although stems can manufacture food for the plant, this function is primarily the role of the leaves. Leaves also help the plant regulate its moisture content and internal temperature by allowing water to evaporate from their surfaces or by wilting, when necessary, to reduce their exposure to sun and air. Leaves come in a huge variety of shapes, sizes, and textures and can occur singly or as one of several leaves attached in a group on a single stalk.

A cluster of leaves at the base of the plant is called a *basal rosette*. Stems and flower stalks rise from this clump of leaves and often die back to the basal rosette at the end of the growing season.

Flowers

You may think that plants form flowers solely for your viewing pleasure (and so you have something to present to your sweetheart on Valentine's Day). But flowers are the reproductive structure of a perennial. The bright, sweet-smelling flower blossom is meant to attract pollinators such as bees, flies, butterflies, birds, moths, and bats. These creatures get a meal of nectar or pollen in exchange for carrying bits of pollen to other flowers in the garden. When a bee brushes pollen from one Shasta daisy onto another — bingo! — pollination occurs.

Very small flowers are often wind-pollinated, producing prodigious amounts of pollen in a hit-or-miss system that greatly affects hay fever sufferers. However, most garden flowers are chosen for their very showy blossoms, which don't cause hay fever.

Flowers have evolved into a vast multitude of different shapes, sizes, and colors to lure and accommodate their various pollinators. Flowers can be held on a single stem or in multiples on spikes; in flattened clusters or loosely branched.

What appears to be a single flower may actually be a cluster of many tiny flowers, forming a *flowerhead*. One example is the daisy, which is called a *composite* because it's composed of two kinds of flowers: the tiny tubular flowers forming the center button and the frill of petals around the outside edge.

Seedheads

After a flower is pollinated, it forms seed. The flower deteriorates — first fading and wilting, and then turning brown and dropping petals. If you don't cut off the dead bloom at this point, most flowers go to seed — that is, form seedpods or capsules. Some seedheads are as attractive as the flowers themselves. If you leave these seedheads on the plant, you can enjoy their beauty long after all the flowers are gone.

Flowers that develop seeds and germinate in your garden are said to *self-sow* or *volunteer*. The baby plants that come up are called *seedlings*.

Some perennials are sterile and don't make viable seed. You can't grow more of these plants from seed, but you can chop the plants up and grow each part into a new plant that's identical to the parent.

Going Perennial

Why grow perennials and not annuals? For two very good reasons: Perennials offer more visual interest than annuals, and (despite what you may think) perennials are actually easier to manage than annuals in the long run.

A tribute to the changing seasons

Unlike static landscapes, perennial flower beds celebrate and, to some extent, choreograph the passing seasons. The institutional annual-flower displays, ever popular in municipal plantings, look exactly the same from the day they're planted until the first blackening frost. In sharp contrast, perennials reflect the passing seasons and are constantly changing and evolving. Tulips and daffodils give way to summer's bounty, and asters and chrysanthemums announce Indian summer.

The ephemeral quality of most perennials is part of their charm. I've heard gardeners say that they refuse to grow the tall bearded iris because it only blooms for a couple of weeks in spring. To me, that reasoning makes about as much sense as forgoing sweet corn because it's only available for a short season in late summer. Tall bearded iris and other transient pleasures restore nature's rhythm to modern lives that are too often confined to a virtual reality of temperature-controlled interiors and silk plants.

Easy to grow — within reason

Most perennials are endlessly forgiving as long as you plant their roots downward and point their leaves toward the light.

In fact, perennials are such versatile plants that a few misconceptions about them have inevitably taken root.

The novice gardener who chooses perennials to avoid having to replant annually is going to be disappointed to discover that many perennials don't survive the three years that, by definition, classify them as perennials. Many perennials are short-lived under any circumstances, and even the long-lived ones only endure when conditions are to their liking.

At a nursery this past spring, a gentleman asked me for advice about a particularly difficult site he had — a dry spot under a shallow-rooted tree where no direct sunlight got through. He wanted me to recommend a perennial so he wouldn't have to spend the money to replant annuals there every year. He also wanted the plant to have evergreen foliage and flowers all summer long. When I finally found a plant that met all these exacting requirements, the man said that he wasn't too crazy about that particular choice and asked me to please show him some other options. He wasn't happy to learn that there were no other options, and I'm sure that, to this day, he thinks I was just being thick-headed.

Some perennials are, indeed, tough and resilient enough to grow in a crack in concrete, even during the hottest and driest summers. A few perennials outlive the gardener who planted them. Old, abandoned homesteads in the American West are often distinguished by non-native flowers still thriving — without a care, mind you — decades after the structures have collapsed.

Most traditional flowers are easy to grow, especially if you keep your expectations realistic. Perennials promise to bring even the most casual gardener endless hours of delight (peppered with occasional moments of frustration as a reality check). Wherever you live and whatever the conditions you have to offer, you can find perennial flowers that can oblige.

A Flower for Every Personality

With all the fervor of a new religious cult, the interest in perennial flowers has taken the gardening world by storm. The craze isn't so surprising when you consider the great variety and diversity these flowers offer the gardener. Perennial gardening has a facet to suit every character type or need:

- ✔ **The Type-A gardener:** People with a competitive disposition can find an outlet for their energies at plant shows and other such contests. They can line their walls with awards and blue ribbons to their heart's content. Every community hosts a plethora of opportunities — from garden-club flower shows to county fairs. Growing winning flowers takes much less time, money, and space than many similar endeavors — say, raising show horses or collecting antique cars.

- ✔ **The pack-rat gardener:** The collector who has run out of shelf space inside the house can turn to the garden for new ground. You can find two general types of perennial collectors: the specialist and the generalist.

  - The *specialist* falls in love with a particular plant and ends up with 150 daylilies (or iris or hostas or — well, you get the point). These folks often have to move to a larger property to accommodate their ever-expanding collections. Most single-flower nurseries have their origins in a collection run amok.

  - The generalist wants one of every flower ever grown. I'm in this category, so I know it well. The if-it's-new-I-want-it crowd attends lectures on botanical explorations to remote parts of the planet, eagerly awaiting each new introduction from the high mountains of Tajikistan or the rain forests of Brazil. Serious garden designers disapprove of the collector's garden because it deteriorates into an unrelated hodgepodge of diverse habitats. Art is not the goal here. Meeting the cultural needs of these many treasures takes precedence.

- ✔ **The therapeutic gardener:** A neighbor of mine is a busy professional whose hectic schedule leaves her few opportunities to relax and indulge in complete calm and quiet. Her perennial garden is her therapy, providing an escape from the demands of clients and family. Puttering around in the garden guarantees fresh air and exercise with compensation that a spa or a gym can't offer. Gardening pays back hard work with a sense of pride and accomplishment — not to mention dazzling displays of color and beauty.

✔ **The nature lover:** This person is stuck in the city or suburbia but longs for the countryside. The nature lover wants critters to liven up the landscape. Every passing bird, bee, and butterfly is invited to drop in for a visit, and some inevitably stay and set up housekeeping. Gardens bring nature "up close and personal" by supplying food and shelter to all manner of wildlife.

✔ **The nonconformist:** Most yards are pretty much the same up and down both sides of the street — lawn, one shade tree, and a few shrubs. A tour of the interiors of these same houses would reveal an entirely different scenario; you would find the varied interests and personalities of the homeowners proudly displayed. Perennial gardening provides the perfect opportunity for public display of the same kind of self-expression. Adding a flower bed is an effective antidote to all the sameness of a suburban street (see Figure 1-2).

Figure 1-2: Adding just a few perennial flowers to an entryway transforms a dull landscape into one that says WELCOME.

You will find that perennial gardening has spilled onto the Internet. Check out the Perennial Plant Association (http:// garden.cas.psu.edu/ppa.html), an organization for landscapers, nurseries, designers, educators, and the general public. If you get really caught up in growing perennials, you may want to join this association yourself. Members have access to an annual symposium, a membership directory for networking, and guides to regional meetings and gardens. A bounty of gardening information is also available at the National Gardening Association's Web site (`http://www.garden.org`). You can find a guide to Web sites of other gardening associations at GardenNet (`http://trine.com/GardenNet/GardenAssn/assnguil.htm`).

Chapter 2

Gardening by Climate: Cooler Areas

*E*very gardener sincerely believes that his or her own climate is the worst on the face of the planet. Although some people offer up southwestern England and Portland, Oregon, as examples of the perfect gardening climate, I strongly suspect that gardeners in these halcyon regions have their own, equally valid complaints.

The cold-climate gardener who has to shovel snow from early fall until late spring isn't likely to feel compassion for the tropical gardener who experiences a few flakes once in five years. Yet that rare snowfall is just the type of record-breaking event that causes the worst damage to gardens.

Find the climate in this chapter or in Chapter 3 that most closely approximates your own and take a look at the sample garden plan I suggest for that climate. The plans are drawn to ¼-inch scale so that you can use an ordinary ruler and carpenter's tape to translate the measurements to the actual flower bed. One inch (2.5 cm) on the plan equals 4 feet (1.2 m) on the ground. Don't spend a great deal of time trying to draw an exact replica of the design; distances can be approximate.

Follow these basic steps to construct your garden:

1. **Mark the outlines of the flower bed.**

2. **Prepare the soil, using the directions in Chapter 6.**

3. **Buy your perennials.**

   Substitutions and modifications are easy. If you can't find a certain plant, or if the perennial in the plan is not appropriate to your climate, simply switch to a different perennial. Choose a plant that's the same height and color as the original suggestion to preserve the character of the design, or break out and pick something entirely different. But make sure that the substitutions you make share the same light, water, and soil requirements as the rest of the flower bed.

4. **Plant your garden.**

Chapter 7 explains how to plant your garden. Chapters 8 through 12 tell you how to care for your garden after it's in the ground.

Choosing What to Grow Based on Where You Live

From time to time, gardeners in every region have to contend with challenges caused by various natural disasters — floods, hurricanes, tornadoes, hail, drought, brush fires, and plagues of locusts, to name a few. But you aren't likely to base your plant choices on these extreme incidents — unless, of course, hail or drought are normal annual occurrences in your region (in which case you'd better give serious thought to defensive gardening — or, better yet, consider moving). Instead, gardeners base plant choices on average conditions.

Unfortunately, averages are almost always deceiving. After all, a plant whose roots are frozen solid and whose petals are on fire is, on average, experiencing mild temperatures. When trying to interpret weather data, you need to know whether a local average temperature of 70° F (21° C) is the result of a never-ending chain of balmy 70° F days or a series of alternating 100° F (38° C) highs and 40° F (4.5° C) lows. Where I live, sorry to say, the latter condition is definitely the case.

Wintertime: Looking beyond the lows

Average low temperatures create a useful guideline, but many factors other than a plant's tolerance to cold determine hardiness. Whether a particular freeze actually damages a plant depends on several factors:

- **What stage of growth the plant is in when the freeze occurs:** Is the plant big enough to take a few hits, or is it still a helpless baby?

- **The length of the cold spell:** They all seem endless, but some cold spells really are longer than others.

- **The windchill factor:** What's the perceived temperature, taking into account the bluster effect?

- **What the weather was like before and after the freeze:** Are you going from hot to cold or from cold to colder?

- **The presence or absence of snow cover:** Believe it or not, plants actually prefer a blanket of snow in winter.

GARDEN JARGON

Zoning out

In an attempt to make some sense of the climate chaos and to help you predict which plants are likely to do well in your region, gardening gurus have created standardized charts, called *zone maps,* mostly based on low temperature averages.

When you pick up a perennial at your local nursery, you're likely to see a zone rating on the label — for example, "Hardy to Zone 5." This zone rating corresponds to an average wintertime low temperature on a particular zone map. For example, according to the United States Department of Agriculture (USDA) Zone Map, a zone 5 perennial can, in general, withstand low temperatures to –20° F. But according to the Western European Plant Hardiness Zone Map, a zone 5 perennial can generally withstand an average winter low of –23° C (which is –10° F!).

Because zone maps vary from place to place, I use average low temperatures (in Celsius and Fahrenheit) throughout this book instead of zone ratings.

Even a hint of frost may be fatal to a tropical or subtropical perennial. Most plants from temperate regions avoid winter by going into a dormant state and indulging in a version of horticultural hibernation, but early and late freezes can catch plants off-guard and kill an otherwise hardy and healthy plant. Winter wetness can also be fatal to plants that demand well-drained soil, which explains why lavender is completely hardy in my garden in relatively dry Denver, Colorado, but not in wetter regions where the temperature doesn't drop as low.

Although most perennials disdain frost, some actually insist on a period of chilling in order to rest and recuperate, regardless of the weather. If deprived of winter cold, such perennials sulk, becoming short-lived or refusing to bloom. For this reason, if you live in a warm-winter climate, you must refrigerate tulips and daffodils for a few weeks before planting them outside.

The many factors that make up your climate

Winter is only one of many elements of climate that affect a plant's success or failure. When a plant is labeled hardy to 30°, for example, you need to know which 30°. Consider the vast differences between San Diego, California, and Miami, Florida — both of which have average winter lows around 30° to 35° F (–1° to –2° C).

✔ San Diego nearly qualifies as a desert, with only 9 inches (23 cm) of rainfall annually, whereas Miami receives a soggy 57 inches (1.45 m) of rain per year.

✔ San Diego is a considerably cooler climate, experiencing only a few days each year when the temperature rises over 90° F (32° C). Miami averages 55 days per year with temperatures over 90° F.

✔ Night temperatures in San Diego and Miami are also quite dissimilar. The record overnight low for Miami in the summer is a warm 70° F (21° C), but you won't catch residents of San Diego out after dark without a sweater.

All the preceding factors profoundly affect the best plant choices for these localities, even though they share the same average low wintertime temperature.

To plan for a garden in your region — a garden that will actu-ally grow, that is — you have to take into account many more factors than low-temperature averages and the length and severity of winters. In addition, consider all the following fac-tors as you plan your perennial garden:

✔ **Different soil types:** Differing soil types influence which perennials are likely to succeed in your garden. Most perennials are surprisingly flexible and adapt content-edly to whatever soil you plant them in, as long as you meet their basic requirements for fertility, water, and drainage. Others are finicky about soil acidity or alkalin-ity. The more extreme your soil, the more restricted your plant choices become.

You can modify any soil to suit a wider range of flowers — but only within limitations. Changing a highly alkaline desert soil into an acid loam isn't impossible, but it is a pain in the azalea. And the solution is usually only tem-porary, anyway. For more details on soil types, check out Chapter 6.

✔ **Average rainfall and drainage:** Perennials vary greatly in their water requirements. Those originating in swamps, ponds, and wet meadows clearly enjoy wet feet (although many such perennials are surprisingly drought tolerant for short periods). However, not all water-lovers can grow in standing water. Many stream-bank natives, for example, need the abundant dissolved oxygen that run-ning water carries. Dry-land perennials can rot from a single heavy rainfall if drainage is poor.

✔ **Average hours and intensity of sunlight:** A plant's sun-light prerequisites can change markedly from one climate to the next. How many hours of sunlight are sufficient depends on the quality and intensity of the light.

You can get a fair idea of the sun's strength in your area by considering how long it takes to get a sunburn. In Denver, where 15 minutes of midday sun fries the aver-age person to a crisp, even sun-worshipping plants are content with only a couple of hours of sunlight each day. Many perennials that need full sun exposure in cooler cli-mates end up begging for protection from the afternoon sun in hot, sunny regions. The reverse is also true. Some shade-lovers can accept full sun when grown in cool, overcast climates, such as in Seattle or London.

✔ **Overnight temperatures:** The high overnight temperatures in some regions can affect the longevity of certain plants more than winter cold. Many traditional perennials don't get the rest they need when hot and humid days are followed by high nighttime temperatures. Some perennials can adapt to extreme summer heat and humidity if the winter is cold enough to stimulate a dormant rest period. However, a few perennials from cool climates can't tolerate heat with high humidity under any circumstance.

✔ **Relative humidity:** The average humidity in your region greatly influences your garden's water needs. Your perennials can dehydrate at astonishing speeds in arid climates but don't dry out so quickly in humid areas. On the other hand, moist air encourages fungal and bacterial diseases. You may not want to use perennials prone to these maladies if the relative humidity in your area routinely keeps pace with the air temperature.

✔ **Air and soil temperature:** Perennials dislike very high air and soil temperatures. They sulk and stop growing when things get toasty, and soil that's too hot is lethal to plant roots.

All the factors that make up your gardening climate are interrelated. For example, relative humidity, sun exposure, and air and soil temperature all help determine an individual plant's water requirements. A plant that never needs a single drop of irrigation in a cool and rainy climate may be perpetually thirsty in an arid region and may insist on supplemental water three times a week.

Cultivating Cold-Climate Perennials

On some winter mornings, would you be less surprised to find polar bears romping through your garden than rabbits or squirrels? Is your garden more likely to sprout Popsicles than perennials?

Extreme cold is the greatest limitation for some gardeners. In regions where winter temperature minimums average between –30° to –40° F (–35° to –40° C) (and occasionally dip even lower than that), where the windchill adds to the arctic effect, and where erratic shifts in heat and cold can occur during any season, you need perennials with the constitution of a junkyard dog.

Only the strong survive

A record-breaking cold spell can damage even the hardiest plants — I've witnessed more than one especially severe winter badly burn or kill seemingly bullet-proof junipers. In addition, rainfall is often unpredictable in cold climates, and summers may be either prone to drought or wet and humid, depending on where you live. The frost-free growing season is often unreasonably short in these climates — lasting only three to four months. Some areas are lucky to get 60 consecutive days without frost.

Gardens in cold-winter climates tend to be high summer gardens. Because the gardening season is short, plants rush to bloom, with most peaking at about the same time. Instead of bemoaning the short season, plan a garden party for mid to late summer and amaze your friends from more temperate climes.

Winter hardiness depends on a number of elements beyond low temperatures. The perfect winter would gradually become colder as the days grew shorter in the fall, stay consistently cold throughout the winter months, and slowly warm up again the following spring. The reality falls far short of this ideal. Summer ends abruptly when a late summer blizzard assaults the garden and knocks down a few tree limbs and power lines. Temperatures jump all over the thermometer, and bitter cold alternates with a few balmy days.

Here are just a few of the ways in which winter's capriciousness can wreak havoc with your perennials:

- Early hard freezes, arriving in fall before your perennials have had time to adjust to cold weather, can cause winter injury.

- A late spring frost can sometimes damage even the most cautious plant.

✔ Snowstorms right smack in the middle of the growing season are most distressing. When such storms occur, many gardeners seriously contemplate a move to warmer climes. Fortunately, midsummer freezes are rare events.

Winter sun and thaw also pose a significant threat to plants. Many plants that don't survive winter die not because they got too cold, but because they warmed slightly on a sunny day and then were unable to readjust quickly enough when frigid temperatures returned. From a plant's point of view, once frozen, it's better to stay frozen.

Snow serves as the down comforter of mulches. A thick layer of snow keeps the ground solidly frozen and unaffected by constantly fluctuating air temperatures. Flowers tucked cozily under this insulating blanket aren't tempted to break dormancy prematurely — they much prefer to hit the snooze button a few times. If an unusually warm spell breaks the winter freeze, you may gratefully throw off your coat, hat, and mittens to revel in the temporary warmth. But the garden that indulges in the horticulture equivalent of throwing off winter garb can't bundle itself back up again when winter inevitably comes back in force.

 Perennials that are only marginally hardy in your region may survive winter if you plant them on the north side of a building. In this normally shady location, plants are least likely to thaw on sunny winter days.

Planning a winter-proof flower bed

 Imagine a flower bed made up of a group of perennials as tough and sturdy as any dandelion, but with some of the most beautiful and graceful blooms available. The garden in Figure 2-1 represents a good plan if your climate has very cold, snowy winters and humid summers, with an annual precipitation greater than 25 inches (63.5 cm). (These weather-proof bruisers are hardy to –40° F [–40° C], but they also do well in climates with warmer low-temperature averages.)

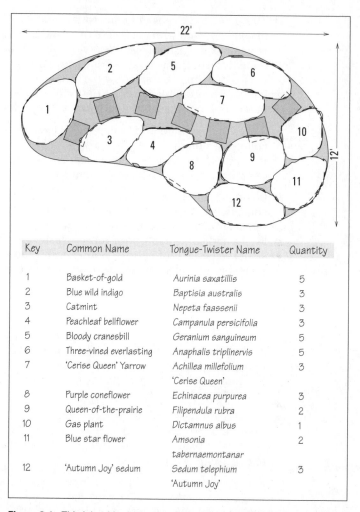

Figure 2-1: This island bed of perennials thrives in a cold-region garden.

Key	Common Name	Tongue-Twister Name	Quantity
1	Basket-of-gold	Aurinia saxatillis	5
2	Blue wild indigo	Baptisia australis	3
3	Catmint	Nepeta faassenii	3
4	Peachleaf bellflower	Campanula persicifolia	3
5	Bloody cranesbill	Geranium sanguineum	5
6	Three-vined everlasting	Anaphalis triplinervis	5
7	'Cerise Queen' Yarrow	Achillea millefolium 'Cerise Queen'	3
8	Purple coneflower	Echinacea purpurea	3
9	Queen-of-the-prairie	Filipendula rubra	2
10	Gas plant	Dictamnus albus	1
11	Blue star flower	Amsonia tabernaemontanar	2
12	'Autumn Joy' sedum	Sedum telephium 'Autumn Joy'	3

Plant this garden in full sun and give it a thorough soaking once a week during the growing season, if rainfall isn't sufficient. This garden rewards you year-round with the following procession of blooms:

✔ This garden awakens in spring with bright yellow basket-of-gold, covered with masses of tiny flowers on spreading mounds of grayish foliage. Basket-of-gold blooms contentedly right through late spring snowfalls. Soft blue clouds of catmint soon follow the basket-of-gold. Tuck a few crocuses or small species tulips in and around both basket-of-gold and catmint for extra spring color.

✔ Spikes of deep blue wild indigo rise above bluish foliage. Following a month of bloom, dark, pea-like pods form at the ends of the stems — leave them on for winter drama or cut to add to dried flower bouquets.

✔ Bloody cranesbill is unabashedly magenta, with handsome foliage that does double duty by turning brilliant red in autumn. 'Cerise Queen' yarrow has finely cut leaves and large, flat-topped flower clusters on long stems — perfect for cutting. Both bloody cranesbill and yarrow are available in more subdued color forms, if you prefer a softer pink.

✔ Gas plant produces loose spikes of showy pink flowers over crisp, thick, green leaflets. White peachleaf bellflower features wide-open blossoms and tall, upright stalks. Long, arching stems of blue star appropriately carry constellations of smoky blue star-shaped flowers. In autumn, the foliage becomes a clear yellow, if an early freeze doesn't burn it.

✔ Summer brings sparkling purple coneflowers with bristly, bright orange centers and queen-of-the-prairie — a large, impressive plant with pink cotton-candy plumes towering above dramatic foliage.

✔ In midsummer, small white star flowers appear amid the linear, silver leaves of pearly everlasting. In late summer, the rounded flowerheads of 'Autumn Joy' sedum open pink and then age to a rust color over waxy, succulent leaves. If an early snow doesn't smash the seedheads, leave them uncut to grace the garden all winter long.

Dressing Up the Drylands

The cold-winter/dry-summer climate encompasses a large area of western North America, including the high plains of the United States and Canada. Summers are devilishly hot,

except at higher elevations. Low winter temperatures average
–20° F (–29° C) and erratic temperature fluctuations can wreak
havoc on the garden and affect plant hardiness.

Within these areas lie a few so-called banana belts where fruit
orchards flourish. A commercial peach and cherry production
near your home is an indication of relatively steady and even
winter temperatures. In these locations, you can safely flaunt
many hardiness recommendations and grow less hardy perennials than gardeners in other areas within your region can.

Some common challenges of this climate include the following:

- ✔ **Generally poor soils:** The dirt in this climate is usually
  stony, sandy, or highly alkaline clay. Humus content is
  very low. (See Chapter 6 for more information about
  soils.)

- ✔ **Notoriously low humidity:** The entire region is exceed-
  ingly dry. Locals tease that you don't even need a towel
  to dry off after you shower.

- ✔ **Unreliable snow cover:** Because of the low humidity,
  snow usually evaporates before it has a chance to soak
  in.

- ✔ **Not enough rain:** The average annual rainfall of 8 to 15
  inches (20 to 38 cm) isn't adequate for traditional perennials without generous supplemental irrigation.

Conserving water with xeriscaping

Water is a scarce and precious resource in these arid regions.
Coping with inevitable shortages has given rise to the
xeriscape movement — combining good horticulture with
water conservation to create flower gardens every bit as lush,
full, and vibrant as those in more temperate climates.

Xeriscape may sound like one of those phony words that des-
perate Scrabble players make up in an attempt to bluff a high
score. But the term actually combines *xeric* (a dry habitat or a
plant from such a place) with *landscape* to create *xeriscape* —
literally, a dry landscape. Unfortunately, xeriscape is easily
mispronounced as "zero-scape," resulting in a complete mis-
understanding. Many folks equate xeriscaping with covering
the ground from house front to curb with rock and gravel —

and they know they don't want that. These gravelscapes unquestionably save water, but xeriscaping advocates much more.

Xeriscape is a system, not a style. A xeriscape can be as formal as Versailles or as casual as a cottage garden. You can't drive up and down the street and pick out the xeriscapes; only the water bill tells the story. Xeriscaping relies on fixing poor soils, grouping together plants with similar needs, mulch, and efficient irrigation. But the most important factor is choosing perennials with low water needs. Many flowers that hail from regions of the world with similar climates do fine on naturally occurring precipitation. In fact, seasonal blazes of flowers are the distinguishing feature of semi-arid regions. Recreating this effect in your garden is only natural.

A few characteristics help you estimate a flower's water needs. Although not 100 percent accurate, these characteristics are good indicators. Most drought-tolerant plants employ one or more of the following adaptations:

- **Succulent leaves:** Fat, fleshy leaves and stems act as water storage tanks. You probably recognize cacti as an example, but 'Autumn Joy' sedum also exhibits this feature.

- **Large roots:** Roots are an underground water storage system. Many prairie and desert natives have massive roots — some reported to weigh as much as a grown man.

- **Silver or gray hairy leaves:** Light colored, fuzzy leaves reflect intense sunlight and shade the leaf surface.

- **Small leaves:** Cacti take this feature to the extreme. The smaller the leaf, the less surface area exposed to drying winds and sunlight.

Planting your own xeriscape

With an abundance of shimmering silvery foliage and lively crayon colors, the garden shown in Figure 2-2 stands up to the harshest summer sunlight and drought.

Put this garden where it will receive at least six hours of direct sunshine each day. The soil doesn't need to be particularly fertile, but it must be well drained. After planting, cover the exposed soil with several inches of mulch. Water deeply whenever the soil dries out until the plants are actively growing, and once or twice a month thereafter or as needed. Chapter 8 helps you determine how often to water your garden.

These rugged plants bring attractive foliage and a long blooming season to the dry flower garden. Leave all the seedheads uncut until spring for a full year of texture and interest. With proper care, this garden rewards you with the following brilliant blooms:

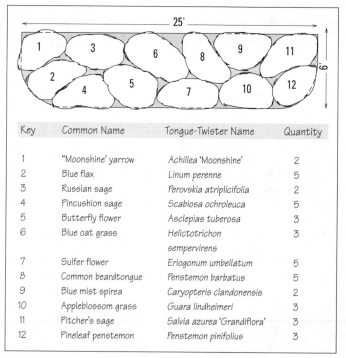

Key	Common Name	Tongue-Twister Name	Quantity
1	"Moonshine' yarrow	Achillea 'Moonshine'	2
2	Blue flax	Linum perenne	5
3	Russian sage	Perovskia atriplicifolia	2
4	Pincushion sage	Scabiosa ochroleuca	5
5	Butterfly flower	Asclepias tuberosa	3
6	Blue oat grass	Helictotrichon sempervirens	3
7	Sulfer flower	Eriogonum umbellatum	5
8	Common beardtongue	Penstemon barbatus	5
9	Blue mist spirea	Caryopteris clandonensis	2
10	Appleblossom grass	Guara lindheimeri	3
11	Pitcher's sage	Salvia azurea 'Grandiflora'	3
12	Pineleaf penstemon	Penstemon pinifolius	3

Figure 2-2: Here is a sample border of perennial flowers for dry-region gardens.

✔ Blue flax is a short-lived perennial that pops up in every nook and cranny to become a filler for the whole garden if you allow it to spread. The silver gray flowers of blue flax complement the lemon yellow tones of 'Moonshine' yarrow nearby.

✔ Acid yellow sulfur flowers age to rust red. Creamy pin-cushion flowers provide a soft bridge next to intense orange butterfly flower. Silvery blue oat grass catches every passing breeze. Russian sage stands at the rear of the bed and sends up steel blue spikes in late summer.

✔ Scarlet common beardtongue and soft orange pineleaf penstemon attract hummingbirds into areas that they don't usually frequent. Appleblossom grass's delicate white blossoms resemble butterflies on slender, arching stems.

✔ Brilliant blue pitcher's sage (also called azure sage), one of the latest flowers to bloom in fall, joins blue mist spirea, a small shrub featuring sky blue whorls that dry to the color of straw. Blue mist spirea's dried flowerheads poke up through winter snows to grace the off-season garden.

Chapter 3

Gardening by Climate: Every Place Else

*I*f you don't own a polar parka, then your climate is probably in this chapter. But check out the numbered list about garden planning as well as the bulleted list on climate factors in Chapter 2 for more guidance on picking your correct climate.

Gardening Where It's Mild and Moist All Year Long

Newcomers to Seattle, Washington, are warned against standing too long in one place lest they start to collect moss on their north side. The same can be said of most of the northwest U.S., British Columbia, and Great Britain. All share a gentle climate where the weather is mild year-round, even though the changing seasons are also clearly defined.

Some characteristics of this type of climate include the following:

- ✔ **Cool summers:** Summers are cool and overcast, punctuated by an occasional spell of bright, sunlit days. When I lived in England, I heard folks comment that there were two days of summer, but those two days were not necessarily in a row.

- ✔ **Mild winters:** Snow falls most winters, but not often enough to make a nuisance of itself. Killing frosts can (and do) sneak down from the arctic, but not with any great regularity. And even then, the temperatures rarely plummet below 0° F (–18° C).

- ✔ **Moderate, steady rainfall:** Rainfall is moderate and conveniently spaced throughout the seasons. Even so, periods of extended drought are not at all uncommon. Resulting water shortages seem like irony in a region with a reputation for being constantly damp and rainy.

Perennial paradise

This moderate, marine climate is a genuine Shangri-La for perennial gardening. Winters are sufficiently cold to satisfy bulbs and other flowers that require a period of chilling. But winters aren't frigid enough to exclude tender choices that can't tolerate an annual arctic freeze.

Mild summers spare flowers the "crispy midsummer stage" that gardens in hot summer regions have to endure. A few flowers don't get adequate sunlight to bloom in these moderate regions, however. Others refuse to open except on sunny days. You may as well leave these sun worshippers to more appropriate climates. For consolation, remind yourself of all the woodland wildflowers, ferns, roses, and rhododendrons that you can grow to perfection.

Pastels for a sparkling island bed

One advantage of living in an overcast climate is that you can safely use even the quietest pastel tones without fearing that the harsh sunlight will wash out the colors. The garden in Figure 3-1 is composed of muted pinks, buttery yellows, lavender, and blue. All these colors glow softly in overcast light.

Locate this island bed in the sunniest section of your property, where it gets at least six hours of unobstructed sunlight each day. Don't fret if clouds get in the way — filtered sunlight is sufficient. Choose a site relatively free of tree roots for ease of preparation and to limit competition between the trees and flowers for water and nutrients. You can place this garden off to one side in an expanse of lawn or surround it on all sides with a mulched path. Build the path wide, so that you can walk freely around the bed to admire the following flowers from every angle.

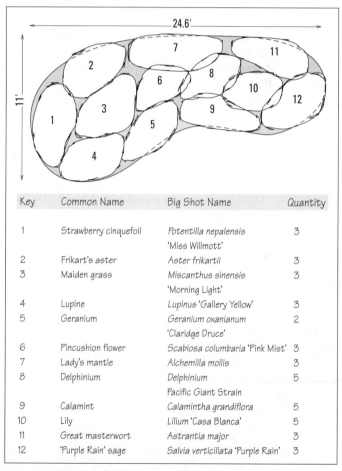

Key	Common Name	Big Shot Name	Quantity
1	Strawberry cinquefoil	Potentilla nepalensis 'Miss Willmott'	3
2	Frikart's aster	Aster frikartii	3
3	Maiden grass	Miscanthus sinensis 'Morning Light'	3
4	Lupine	Lupinus 'Gallery Yellow'	3
5	Geranium	Geranium oxanianum 'Claridge Druce'	2
6	Pincushion flower	Scabiosa columbaria 'Pink Mist'	3
7	Lady's mantle	Alchemilla mollis	3
8	Delphinium	Delphinium Pacific Giant Strain	5
9	Calamint	Calamintha grandiflora	5
10	Lily	Lilium 'Casa Blanca'	5
11	Great masterwort	Astrantia major	3
12	'Purple Rain' sage	Salvia verticillata 'Purple Rain'	3

Figure 3-1: This island bed features perennials that thrive in places like Seattle, Washington, and London, England.

- Delphiniums are the signature flower of the cool-summer perennial garden. They tower to impressive heights — each stately spike crowded with flat, open-faced blossoms. You may want to stake these plants so they don't fall face down in the mud (a much less elegant repose). Bold but elegant 'Casablanca' lilies stand up to the imposing delphinium with large, gleaming white flowers that send their spicy fragrance throughout the garden.

- Another star performer in the cool-summer climate is the graceful lupine. The individual flowers are quite distinctive, looking like little Dutch wooden shoes attached by their heels to each flower spike.

- Whorls of tiny lavender blossoms grace candelabra-like stems of 'Purple Rain' sage, contrasting sweetly with neighboring masterwort's delicate pink blossoms.

- The white and green variegated foliage of calamint has a strong, minty aroma and small, bright pink, tubular flowers that play off 'Claridge Druce' geranium, with its grayish green foliage and lilac pink blossoms.

- Pincushion flower is aptly named, as each individual flower looks like a pincushion sitting on a lacy doily. Nearby lady's mantle, often grown solely for its heavily folded foliage, has an equally attractive froth of chartreuse flowers.

- 'Miss Willmott' cinquefoil has strawberry-like leaves and cherry pink flowers. The subtle variegation of 'Morning Light' maiden grass adds a touch of grace and can provide an accent to the winter landscape if left in the garden.

Growing Perennials in Warm, Dry Maritime Climates

If a flower-gardening paradise exists, the mild maritime climate of parts of California approaches it. Moderated by the ocean's influence, this region suffers no extremes of heat or cold to test a plant's endurance. Much as in a greenhouse environment, cool and misty conditions prevail at all seasons.

Frosts are infrequent in most maritime regions and almost unheard of in some (such as the southern parts of the California coast). The farther you travel inland from the sea or toward the Poles, or the higher you climb in elevation, the more likely you are to experience regular winter frosts. But even these frosts aren't of the killer arctic nature. The temperature rarely dips much below 30° F (–1° C). Summers are equally mild, dominated by foggy mornings and humid sea breezes. A few heat lovers don't get adequate sunshine, but most perennials thrive in this benevolent climate — as long as they get enough water.

Water everywhere, but . . .

Ah, water — the one shortcoming in regions that would otherwise approach true gardener's paradise. Scarce rainfall is a reality for many coastline communities. Their green lushness is an illusion created by liberal irrigation with imported water. Today, this scarce resource is running out. Water shortages and periodic rationing are increasingly common in all arid and semi-arid regions around the world.

The wise maritime gardener plans for water shortages by choosing from the large number of perennials that need little or no irrigation to prosper.

Planning for mild but thirsty climates

Figure 3-2 shows a garden plan for a climate that's mild year-round, with an annual rainfall below 25 inches (64 cm). Consider a garden like this one if you live in a region that's similar to Santa Barbara, California.

The walk in Figure 3-2 permits ever-changing perspectives and views as it meanders through the flower bed. Use brick or stone for permanence, or choose gravel (with its satisfying crunch underfoot) for a more casual setting.

The plan in Figure 3-2 comprises drought tolerant perennials that can survive with only occasional supplemental water. For this garden, I chose a tough group of plants that can withstand salt-laden gales as well as seasonal, drying desert winds. All these flowers bloom for a long season, and most have evergreen foliage.

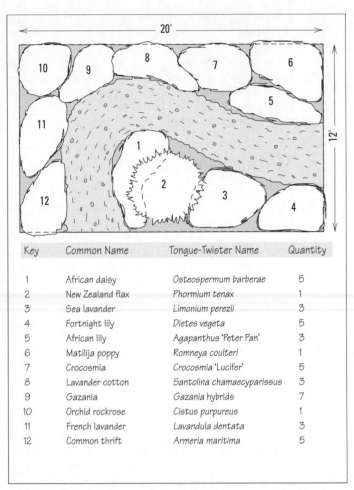

Key	Common Name	Tongue-Twister Name	Quantity
1	African daisy	Osteospermum barberae	5
2	New Zealand flax	Phormium tenax	1
3	Sea lavender	Limonium perezii	3
4	Fortnight lily	Dietes vegeta	5
5	African lily	Agapanthus 'Peter Pan'	3
6	Matilija poppy	Romneya coulteri	1
7	Crocosmia	Crocosmia 'Lucifer'	5
8	Lavender cotton	Santolina chamaecyparissus	3
9	Gazania	Gazania hybrids	7
10	Orchid rockrose	Cistus purpureus	1
11	French lavender	Lavandula dentata	3
12	Common thrift	Armeria maritima	5

Figure 3-2: This bed of perennials is perfect for gardeners who live in coastal or inland-coastal regions of the world.

✔ Not for the timid, New Zealand flax dominates the garden with red, sword-shaped leaves that can reach 9 feet (nearly 3 meters). Substitute Phormium tenax 'Bronze Baby', 'Dark Delight', or another dwarf hybrid where a shorter form seems more appropriate. Smoky lavender African daisies take on a sultry air when planted next to the purplish red fans of the flax.

✔ Sea lavender features large, loose clusters of purple flowers standing high above shiny green foliage. White iris-like blossoms of fortnight lily echo the color of sea lavender, with purple spots on their upper petals and yellow spots on the lower.

✔ Stately Matilija poppy matches the scale of the flax at 8 feet (2.4 m) tall, with salad-plate-sized white crimped poppies with golden centers rising above deeply cut sage green leaves.

✔ 'Peter Pan' is a dwarf African lily only 18 inches (45 cm) tall and long blooming, with dark blue flower clusters and evergreen straplike foliage. You don't have to clap your hands to bring this fairy-tale perennial to life!

✔ Fiery 'Lucifer' really sparks things up with bolts of bright scarlet, tubular flowers dancing like flames among stiffly upright, narrow leaves. Silvery and aromatic lavender cotton and sea lavender cool the flames, their blossoms serving as an added bonus.

✔ Any gazania is compatible in this arrangement, but my favorite (if you can find it) has soft, pink daisies and silver leaves.

✔ Orchid rockrose is a compact shrub that has single, purplish, roselike flowers. Each delicately wrinkled petal is accented at the base with a red spot.

✔ Compact common thrift has cheerful pompoms for flowerheads, which it carries on tall stems over grasslike tufts of foliage. Common thrift blooms almost all year and is available in white, rose pink, or wine red. Plant either a mix of colors or all one variety, whichever you prefer.

Creating Steamy Subtropical Gardens

Subtropical regions experience mild, wet winters and hot, humid summers. The deep south of the U.S. has these conditions. When the winter-weary head to the balmy subtropics, some folks are disappointed to find that many of their old garden favorites can't make the journey with them. Most traditional perennials originate in cooler climates and require a period of winter rest to bounce back hearty and vigorous the following spring. The lack of reliable chilling, coupled with relentless year-round humidity and consistently high night-time low temperature averages, takes its toll on plants that aren't adapted to those conditions.

Still, gardeners new to the subtropics need not despair. Although many dependable cooler-clime standbys (such as peonies, bleeding hearts, delphiniums, bearded iris, lupines, and lady's mantle) do wimp out from the endless heat and humidity, the trade-off is an abundance of tender treasures that you can set free from the conservatory or the windowsill to take up permanent residence in the garden. Extravagantly exotic bulbs — stately amaryllis, sultry Lily of the Nile (aga-panthus), Crocosmia, elegant fortnight lily (dietes), gladiolas, and fragrant crinum — spread like weeds in the subtropics . . . to the genuine envy of gardeners in frostier climates.

It's not the heat; it's the humidity

Periods of very heavy rainfall alternate with prolonged dry spells in these regions, so plants must be able to contend with both extremes. Soil types range from nearly perfect, fertile, well-drained loam to sticky, heavy clay and pockets of pure sand, and from overly acidic to highly alkaline.

Where rainfall is heavy and drainage is poor, amending the soil thoroughly and building raised beds are critical to suc-cessful perennial gardening. Most perennials can't tolerate wet feet for long and may rot if left standing in water puddles.

In general, the same perennials bloom earlier in the year and are shorter-lived when they are grown in warmer climates. Perennials also tend to be taller and less sturdy in the sub-tropical garden than their counterparts grown in cold-weather climates. Whenever one is available, choose a dwarf variety, because it's less likely to flop over without staking. Frequent division — as often as once a year — helps many types main-tain their vigor.

Planning a subtropical garden

For the garden in Figure 3-3, I've chosen a tough group of perennials that laugh off summer's muggiest heat. This mix of wildflowers and traditional perennials include several that, if you regularly *deadhead* (pluck off the dying blooms), bloom for most of the year. Give this garden plan a try if your winters are mild and wet and your summers are hot and humid.

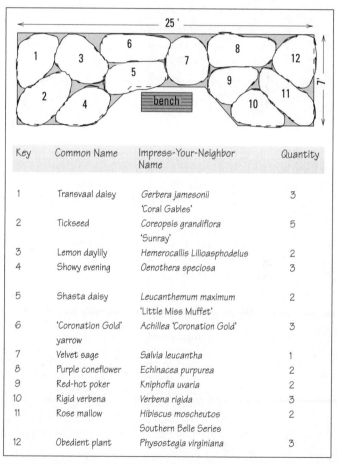

Key	Common Name	Impress-Your-Neighbor Name	Quantity
1	Transvaal daisy	Gerbera jamesonii 'Coral Gables'	3
2	Tickseed	Coreopsis grandiflora 'Sunray'	5
3	Lemon daylily	Hemerocallis Lilioasphodelus	2
4	Showy evening	Oenothera speciosa	3
5	Shasta daisy	Leucanthemum maximum 'Little Miss Muffet'	2
6	'Coronation Gold' yarrow	Achillea 'Coronation Gold'	3
7	Velvet sage	Salvia leucantha	1
8	Purple coneflower	Echinacea purpurea	2
9	Red-hot poker	Kniphofia uvaria	2
10	Rigid verbena	Verbena rigida	3
11	Rose mallow	Hibiscus moscheutos Southern Belle Series	2
12	Obedient plant	Physostegia virginiana	3

Figure 3-3: The perennials in this garden thrive in heat and summer humidity.

Some tips for growing and maintaining the flower bed in Figure 3-3 follow:

✔ Unless your site is very fast draining, raise the bed at least 1 foot (30 cm) higher than ground level and fill the box with a sandy soil mix. Plan to irrigate this garden deeply once a week during long dry spells. (For tips on how and when to water, see Chapter 8.)

✔ Plant this subtropical garden in the fall or, at the very latest, in early winter. You want to give these newly transplanted perennials several months to become settled and establish strong roots before they have to deal with excessive summer heat.

✔ Over the winter, lay down a thick, loose blanket of mulch (see Chapter 13) to protect frost-tender perennials like velvet sage and Transvaal daisies.

✔ In late winter, give the bed a thorough cleaning and cut back old, tired foliage to get everything off to a new start. If any of the perennials become mildewed during the growing season, cut them down to the tuft of leaves at the base of the plant (see Chapter 10), and the new foliage generally comes up free of mildew.

The pastel tones in this garden balance and soften the bright accents of scarlet hibiscus, golden yarrow, and coreopsis.

✔ By late spring, the icy white petals of 'Little Miss Muffet' (a dwarf Shasta daisy) open to reveal clear yellow centers. 'Coral Gables' is a soft orange variety of the Transvaal daisy.

✔ The golden plate-sized flowerheads of 'Coronation Gold' yarrow first appear in late spring and continue for several months. The starry flowers of 'Sunray' tickseed is a lustrous yellow that stops just short of orange.

✔ If you like really big flowers, you're going to love rose mallows. Their oversized blossoms look like they're made of crepe paper. A daintier flower, showy evening primrose produces frosty pink cups with yellow centers for most of the summer. Always stately and regal, the tall flower spikes of red-hot poker rise dramatically above bold, linear foliage.

✔ Sunshine-colored lemon daylilies brighten the midsummer doldrums. But when silvery velvet sage and rosy rigid verbena begin to bloom, you know that fall is not far off.

Planting Perennials in the Scorching Desert

Mild winters distinguish the warm deserts of the southwestern U.S. from the cold drylands. Snow isn't unheard of in this region, but temperatures rarely stay below freezing for long. The mild winters are what attract people to these otherwise-harsh regions (and probably few would stay if they were subjected to a summer without air conditioning!).

Warm deserts share one universal characteristic: Soil and air temperatures are high. Summer heat is relentless enough to melt blacktop, at times shutting down major airports. Soil temperature can be 100° F (38° C) — even 4 inches (10 cm) underground. Few habitats on earth seem as inhospitable to the traditional perennial garden as the desert. But these apparent wastelands have another, more exuberant side. Every so often, rain falls at just the right time to produce an unequaled floral display. Local tourist boards and chambers of commerce host wildflower hotlines at peak seasons to track these short-lived events. Admirers from near and far drop whatever they're doing to go witness the desert in a blaze of color.

Desert soils

Soil types range from pockets of wonderfully fertile soil to nearly pure gravel or heavy clay. Most soils are highly alkaline and some are also quite salty. Desert soils tend to be deficient in decaying organic matter — typically containing only 0.5 to 1 percent. Native vegetation copes with this moisture and nutritional dearth by growing sparsely, spacing themselves widely apart. In the garden — where you want a dense, lush look — amending the soil compensates for the extra competition (see Chapter 6 for tips on amending your soil).

Rainfall is scarce and irregular throughout the warm desert regions. None of these areas receives more than 10 inches (25 cm) annually. Moisture evaporates from the soil faster than rain falls. The key to perennial gardening in this arid climate is to shelter the flower bed from the harsh elements so that it doesn't dry out so quickly.

The oasis garden

Reflecting the desert's occasional explosion of color, the oasis garden in Figure 3-4 features a tough and rugged selection of perennials. All are drought tolerant and tough as nails, but they can still use a little help to look their best in this harsh climate.

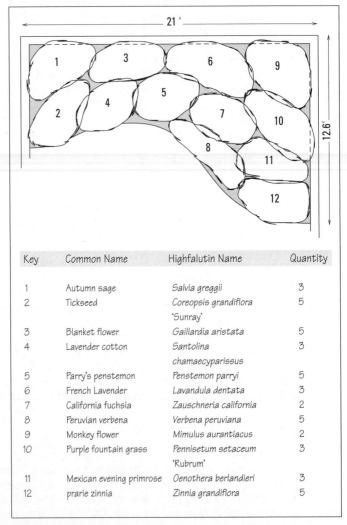

Key	Common Name	Highfalutin Name	Quantity
1	Autumn sage	Salvia greggii	3
2	Tickseed	Coreopsis grandiflora 'Sunray'	5
3	Blanket flower	Gaillardia aristata	5
4	Lavender cotton	Santolina chamaecyparissus	3
5	Parry's penstemon	Penstemon parryi	5
6	French Lavender	Lavandula dentata	3
7	California fuchsia	Zauschneria california	2
8	Peruvian verbena	Verbena peruviana	5
9	Monkey flower	Mimulus aurantiacus	2
10	Purple fountain grass	Pennisetum setaceum 'Rubrum'	3
11	Mexican evening primrose	Oenothera berlandieri	3
12	prarie zinnia	Zinnia grandiflora	5

Figure 3-4: In dry, desert regions, a garden is an oasis.

Place this garden in a courtyard surrounded by a low wall to protect the flowers from sun and drying winds. Or put the garden behind a shelter belt or windbreak of trees and shrubs. Follow these steps to plant and maintain this flower bed:

1. **Plant when the worst of summer's heat is waning.**

   The best time to plant perennials in this climate is early to mid fall.

2. **Amend the soil so that it drains freely but doesn't dry out too quickly.**

3. **After planting, spread several inches of fibrous organic mulch or gravel between the plants.**

4. **Water regularly until the perennials have doubled in size.**

   When the plants are growing strongly, soak the bed once a month in winter and only as often as needed in summer. Always water thoroughly to encourage deep rooting. Water at night or install drip irrigation so that water isn't wasted by evaporation.

The vibrant scarlets, purples, and yellows of the following perennials ensure that the intense sunlight of this climate doesn't wash out this garden's brilliance:

- As its name suggests, autumn sage blooms in fall and winter and is available in pink, coral, purplish red, red, or white. Any of these choices complement this garden, but choose red if you want to attract hummingbirds.

- If you pluck off dying blooms regularly, compact 'Sunray' coreopsis overflows with ragged-edged golden daisies for a very long blooming season.

- Blanket flower, a large burgundy daisy with gilded edges, is set off by the tidy silver mounds of lavender cotton (which appears to be dotted with yellow buttons when in bloom) and the spires of shocking-pink flowers on Parry's penstemon.

- French lavender sends up purplish flower spikes nearly year-round. As if trying to steal the spotlight, attention-grabbing California fuchsia's showy, tubular, scarlet flowers arch above grayish foliage. In the foreground, clusters of rosy pink Peruvian verbena flowers bloom so profusely that they nearly obscure the plant's foliage.

✔ Unlike Mimulus aurantiacus, most monkey flowers like plenty of water, so ask for this plant by its botanical name to make sure that you get the one that likes dry conditions.

✔ Purple fountain grass adds a sense of grace and movement to the garden. Mexican evening primrose refuses to stay put. It comes up everywhere, but its silky pink cups make it a welcome pest. Next door, prairie zinnia, a native of the American southwest, sports little bright yellow daisies.

Chapter 4

Easygoing Favorites with Sunny Dispositions

*F*lowers and sunshine are natural friends. After all, plants need sun to make their food. (Remember photosynthesis from high-school biology?) Although plants that hail from woodland habitats prefer a shady location and perhaps some SPF–14 sunblock, the majority of common perennials love to bask in the sun. This chapter concentrates on these common, sun-loving perennials. (For more on gardening in shade, see Chapter 5.)

Combing through the hundreds of sun-loving perennials to decide which ones to include in this chapter was not an easy task. I grow every flower I can get my hands on, and choosing among them is about as difficult as picking a favorite child. I'm crazy about all my perennials, even though, on different days of the week and at different seasons, some clearly stand above the rest. To narrow down the selection process, this chapter includes only the following (with a few exceptions):

✔ **Perennials that grow in a wide variety of conditions and climates:** Every perennial is easy to grow somewhere, but that somewhere may be very exacting (see the sidebar, "Catering to your climate"). A plant that grows like a weed in a desert region is probably impossible to grow in a cool, damp climate without a greenhouse. But the flowers in this chapter have a wide range of tolerance, as far as climate is concerned.

🖙 **Perennials that are easy to grow:** The most widely adapted perennials, the old favorites that I call traditional perennials, have long ago had their fussiness bred out of them. You don't have to do somersaults and handsprings to keep the plants in this chapter alive and performing up to reasonable expectations.

🖙 **Perennials that are easy to locate:** You can find most of the plants in this chapter at your local nurseries and garden centers.

Too Much of a Good Thing

Perennials that are considered to need "full sun" exposure don't necessarily require sunshine all day long. In hot, desert climates, for example, even the most sun-loving plant may need a bit of afternoon shade to cool down. If you live in a very hot, dry region, try to plant these perennials where they can get plenty of sunshine in the morning, but where a wall, tree, or other structure casts sufficient shade to protect them from the intense afternoon heat.

Subtropical climates can be tricky because of humidity. Hot, muggy climates tend to be much more restrictive than hot, dry regions. In a hot and arid region, you can place a plant that requires cool temperatures in the shade and water it often, but you can't do much to reduce high humidity coupled with intense heat. I've indicated in the text which perennials are most sensitive to heat combined with humidity. In some areas, these plants are grown as annuals, planted in the fall to bloom the next spring. Check with local nurseries and gardeners in your own region to find out their experience with any plant you're uncertain of.

Sun-Loving Perennials

An average of five to six hours of sun a day keeps the perennials in the following list fit and healthy, although most will settle for less sunlight without making too much of a fuss. Look for the term partial shade to find perennials that may need a bit more protection from intense afternoon sun.

Catering to your climate

When you get to the extreme climate limits of perennial gardening — the subtropics and regions with permafrost and polar bears — the number of traditional perennials you can grow is considerably reduced, compared with the more moderate areas.

Perennial gardening has its roots in England, Western Europe, and the northeastern United States, so the flowers that are most compatible to these regions are the ones that have become part of the heritage. The bulk of the plants listed in this chapter reflect this trend, but I have included a few perennials from off the beaten path. Some are subtropical plants that are often grown as annuals in cooler climates. A few are desert relatives of familiar flowers, and a number are plants newly introduced to the nursery trade.

See Chapters 2 and 3 for a discussion on the particulars of how climates and temperatures affect what perennials you can grow.

Because the common names of perennials vary so much from place to place, the following list is arranged alphabetically according to the more specific (if clunkier) botanical name. (Refer to Chapter 1 for an explanation of botanical versus common names.)

- **Common yarrow** (*Achillea millefolium*): This perennial is absolutely easy-care, except for its wandering tendencies. The flowerheads are large, flat clusters of tiny daisies on long, straight stems — excellent for cutting or drying. The foliage is dark green, very fine, ferny, and aromatic when crushed. 'Cerise Queen' is bright, rosy red. 'Paprika' opens red and fades to burnished gold. The Galaxy Series includes soft pastels, such as pale yellow and salmon tones.

Common yarrow grows in spreading mats and can be a bit of a pest if you let it overrun less aggressive companions. The plant is less floppy and better behaved in dry, well-drained, infertile soil. Fertilize it infrequently and lightly. Divide it annually to control spread or to propagate.

Cut the stems down to within a few inches of the ground after blooming is finished. No winter protection is necessary. Common yarrow is short-lived in hot and humid areas. It enjoys hot daytime temperatures but prefers cool nights. Common yarrow can withstand average wintertime temperatures as low as –40° F (–40° C).

A relative of common yarrow, 'Coronation Gold' yarrow (*Achillea* 'Coronation Gold') grows 2 to 3 feet (60 to 90 cm) tall; has ferny, gray green foliage; and produces dozens of deep yellow flowers over several months.

✔ **Japanese windflower** (*Anemone hybrida*): Japanese windflowers prefer partial shade, except in cool climates, where they can withstand full sun. In autumn, sprays of delicate pink, deep rose, or sparkling white flowers dance above light- to dark-green grapelike foliage. 'Honorine Jobert' is bright white with yellow centers and dependably produces many flowers. 'September Charm' is rose pink on the inside of the petals, darker on the reverse.

All parts of Japanese windflower are poisonous if eaten in large amounts.

Plant Japanese windflowers in deep, fertile soil with plenty of moisture. In cold regions, protect these plants over the winter with a heavy layer of mulch. They can become invasive, especially in sandy soils. Taller varieties can flop without support. This plant isn't a good choice for a hot, humid, mild-winter climate. But it is handy where wintertime averages don't dip below –30° F (–34° C).

✔ **Common thrift** (*Armeria maritima*): This plant looks like a cluster of drumsticks. In the springtime, tubular blossoms are packed into tight balls and held upright on stiff, straight stems above a tussock of grassy foliage. Diverse varieties are available, from little rock garden miniatures to robust, 1-foot-tall 'Ruby Glow' and 'Splendens'. The pink shades vary from soft and delicate to screaming magenta to almost red.

This plant's only requirement is fast drainage; common thrift is otherwise tough as nails. It tolerates salt, pure sand, and drought.

The foliage of common thrift is evergreen except in extreme cold. In hot and humid climates, this plant appreciates shade from afternoon sun. Remove spent flowerheads to encourage continued blossoming. My plants bloom on and off all summer after their initial spring burst. Common thrift grows in any region and can withstand average wintertime temperatures as low as –40° F (–40° C).

✔ **Frikart's aster** (*Aster frikartii*): An international celebrity, this aster was developed in Switzerland early in the 20th century. It produces masses of blue daisies from midsummer until frost. Butterflies love it. Individual plants are long-lived and carefree. Two varieties are widely sold: 'Mönch' has darker blue flowers and never needs staking; 'Wonder of Staffa' is almost indistinguishable from its sibling.

This plant is not fussy about soil — mine is happy in heavy clay — and is tolerant of both heat and humidity. Most sources report limited winter hardiness. Plants in my Colorado garden have survived –20° F (–28° C) through several winters without damage. However, wet winters may be fatal at much higher temperatures. My plants don't get a winter mulch, but this may actually improve hardiness by insuring that they dry out completely. A winter mulch may be helpful if the soil is well-drained.

A relative of Frikart's aster, New England asters (*Aster novae-angliae*) 'Alma Potschke', 'Hella Lacy', 'Purple Dome', and 'September Ruby' are big plants that give a spectacular fall show These varieties are prone to developing "bare legs," so place them behind other, shorter perennials for camouflage.

✔ **Summer daisies** (*Dendranthema*): Like The Artist Formerly Known as Prince, summer daisies used to be called chrysanthemums until the botanists needed something to do and got busy changing their names. To confuse things further, these flowers don't really have a proper common name and are usually referred to by their variety names. The best known variety, 'Clara Curtis', is pink; 'Mary Stoker' has buff-colored daisies. All varieties have grayish green, strongly aromatic foliage.

Touching the leaves can cause a skin rash in sensitive individuals.

Give summer daisies full sun in any soil except soggy. The fragrant flowers are great as cut flowers. Cut a few inches from the tips of each stem several times before midsummer to create more compact plants and later blooms. This plant grows in any climate but the very coldest; it's hardy to an average wintertime low of –30° F (–34° C).

My only complaint with summer daisies is that they spread like wildfire in fertile soil and need dividing annually to stop them from taking over the whole flower bed. But tough is an asset in some situations, and no chrysanthemum is tougher.

✔ **Purple coneflower** (*Echinacea purpurea*): Large, purplish pink daisies with bristly orange centers contradict the old adage that pink and orange always clash. Foliage is large, coarse, and dark green. Purple coneflower is a good cut flower, and butterflies find it irresistible. It blooms for a very long period, from early summer to frost. After the petals fall, the cone is attractive in dried arrangements.

Unaffected by heat and humidity or winter cold, these tough plants are very adaptable, and you can grow purple coneflowers successfully almost anywhere. They're hardy to an average winter low of –40° F (–40° C).

Don't fertilize the soil too much, or the plants may flop over and require staking. Grow them in any soil except wet and poorly drained. Although purple coneflower tolerates short periods of drought, it is happier with regular watering.

✔ **Blanket flower** (*Gaillardia aristata*): In colors so loud they'll rattle your windows, blanket flowers bloom from spring to fall with concentric circles of red and yellow. But like most perennials that bloom for a very long season, blanket flowers tend to be short-lived. They strew their seeds around, but their progeny are usually quite changed in appearance from mom and dad. I replace dead plants each spring and am grateful when any of the previous season's crop survive the winter.

Handling the leaves of this plant may cause skin rashes in sensitive individuals, so wear gloves as a precaution.

Blanket flowers grow anywhere — even on sand dunes in Florida. They are cold-hardy practically to the Canadian tundra (withstanding wintertime lows of –50° F [–46° C]) and appear everywhere in between. In addition, this plant is completely drought tolerant in any climate. Plant blanket flowers in any well-drained soil in full sun — it blooms the first year from seed.

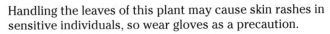

✔ **Appleblossom grass** (*Gaura lindheimeri*): Appleblossom-like flowers dangle on long, willowy stems. The flowers are white with shrimp-pink anthers, lower petals, and stems — from a distance, the overall effect is a pink cloud.

Increasingly popular, this delicate and airy plant has a really rugged constitution. Appleblossom grass is hardier than anyone first suspected, surviving temperatures well below 0° F (–18° C) in well-drained soil and full sun or dappled shade. It's native to regions with plentiful rainfall

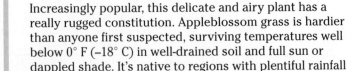

but is also completely drought tolerant in the driest part of my xeric garden. When other desert natives wilt and dry up, appleblossom grass is still going strong. This plant also tolerates extreme heat and humidity.

✔ **Bloody cranesbill** (*Geranium sanguineum*): Very long-blooming and adaptable, bloody cranesbill grows in a loosely mounded form and sports attractive leaves that turn crimson in fall. The simple, open-faced flowers are a strident magenta, held several inches above the foliage. If magenta is too strong a color for your tastes, choose one of the softer varieties. 'Album' is white; *Geranium sanguineum striatum* is pale pink with dark veining.

Plant bloody cranesbill in any soil except the wettest. It can spread far too rapidly in fertile, moist soil and is generally better behaved when kept a little stressed. Thoroughly drought tolerant, bloody cranesbill is also successful in subtropical climates. Although it does grow in dry shade, it produces more blooms in a sunny location. Flowering is heaviest in the spring, but bloody cranesbill blooms sporadically throughout the summer. This plant is hardy to –30° F (–34° C).

✔ **Transvaal daisy** (*Gerbera jamesonii*): Tender daisies grown as annuals outside their hardiness range, Transvaal daisies perform best in hot, humid regions where rainfall is high. They come in a rainbow of colors — white, cream, yellows, apricot, orange, pink, and red — in single and double forms. Each flower is held singly on a strong stem, poised elegantly above low foliage rosettes.

Buy the small seedling size for transplanting into the garden. The large, lush florists' pots don't have a good survival rate.

Transvaal daisies like plenty of water and well-drained soil. Plant in sandy soil well-amended with humus or in raised beds. Let the soil dry out briefly between waterings. This plant may die to ground when temperatures dip below freezing, but it usually returns in spring. Average wintertime lows down to 10° F (–12° C) are acceptable.

✔ **Daylily** (*Hemerocallis hybrids*): The daylily's dazzling trumpets are open for only one day, but are indispensable for the midsummer garden. Daylilies send up new flowers every day for two to three weeks. Hundreds of varieties are available, from pale yellow and orange to red, pink, and purple. All but the deep reds and purples have sherbety undertones. Size is variable, from 12-inch (30-cm) tall miniatures to 4-foot (1.2-m) tall giants, and everything in between. The foliage is green and grasslike, and the flowers are sometimes fragrant.

Most varieties prefer full sun, but reds and purples fade less if they have afternoon shade in hot regions. Give daylilies rich, fertile soil and plenty of water. They happily grow in soggy soils in cold climates. In hot, humid regions, too much water promotes diseases.

Daylilies face the sun, so always place them where you can see their faces. Pick evergreen types for hot, humid, warm-winter climates. Where winters are severe, choose dormant varieties. Check with local daylily societies for the best selections for your area.

✔ **Shasta daisy** (*Leucanthemum maximum*): An indispensable old-fashioned favorite, Shasta daisies are impressive, large white daisies with golden yellow centers. Many forms are available, from simple, rather formal daisies to shaggy doubles. 'Alaska' is the hardiest selection, 'Cobham Gold' is creamy yellow, and 'Alaya' is heavily fringed.

Grow this plant in fertile, well-drained soil. It needs regular water during the growing season but is intolerant of winter wet. Tall varieties flop over if they aren't staked. Cut stems back to within a few inches of the ground when blooming stops. Divide annually in hot, humid climates and pinch stems early in the season to create a bushier plant. Shasta daisy is hardy to –40° F (–40° C).

✔ **Sea lavender** (*Limonium latifolium*): You wouldn't guess what a tough constitution this plant has by looking at it. A delicate haze of tiny lavender flowers fills the air above substantial, dark green foliage. The flowers dry on their stems and hold up almost indefinitely. Sea lavender is a florist's favorite, cut or dried. Leave some stems uncut for winter interest.

Sea lavender is undaunted by salty soils or salt spray. It grows in any soil in cool climates but must have fast draining soil where it's hot and humid, or it may succumb to crown rot. It's equally happy with regular water or very little. Full sun is best in cold climates; afternoon shade is better in hot, humid regions. Cut it to the ground in spring. This plant is hardy to –40° F (–40° C).

✔ **Lupine** (*Lupinus hybrids*): Reliable and easy in cool climates, lupine is unfortunately finicky elsewhere. This perennial comes in a wide array of colors — white, yellow, orange, red, blue, lavender, purple, pink, and two-tones. The substantial flower stalks are 1 to 2 feet (30 to 60 cm) tall over bushy clumps of dark green palm-shaped leaves. It blooms for eight to ten weeks if you cut the spent flower stalks back to the basal rosette.

Eating any part of a lupine plant can cause vomiting, irritation of the mouth and throat, and abdominal discomfort.

Although lupines are utterly intolerant of heat, whether humid or dry, they are definitely worth growing as an annual in hot, humid, mild-winter climates. Plant in late fall for spring blooms. Lupines in my garden are occasionally spectacular, and a real disappointment other years. The successful years are worth the wait. Give them well-drained, moist soil that you've amended with plenty of humus. Lupines are hardy to –30° F (–34° C).

✔ **Maltese cross** (*Lychnis chalcedonica*): An old-fashioned cottage garden favorite, Maltese cross has brilliant scarlet flowerheads. The individual flowers are cross-shaped and carried in rounded clusters at the top of tall, stately stems. It's easy to grow but is usually short-lived. Maltese cross scatters its seeds around, and some of the seeds do grow into new plants. White, pink, and salmon forms are also available.

Give Maltese cross any well-drained soil in full sun. The lower leaves may become brown during dry spells. Hide these "bare legs" behind other flowers. Deadhead routinely to promote continuous blooming and divide clumps every two to three years to maintain vigor. This plant may become a nuisance if all the flowerheads are allowed to set seed. Maltese cross is hardy to –40° F (–40° C).

✔ **Bee balm** (*Monarda didyma*): Available in varieties of pink, white, blue, violet, purple, and scarlet, bee balm's flowers look something like raggedy, mop-head daisies. All parts of the plant are deliciously aromatic, with a scent reminiscent of Earl Grey tea. The green foliage is mintlike, slightly toothed, narrow, and pointed. Clumps can spread invasively, but the runners are shallow and easy to pull out.

Bee balm prefers cool climates and is not a good choice for hot, muggy, or desert regions. (Bee balm can withstand wintertime lows as cold as –30° F [–34° C].) Give it regular, even moisture and rich soil. Spread a thick blanket of organic mulch beneath the plants to help maintain these conditions. Bee balm always comes down with powdery mildew late in the growing season. When the mildew becomes more than you can bear to look at, cut the plants down to the ground. They always recover and grow healthy new foliage for me.

✔ **Ozark sundrop** (*Oenothera macrocarpa*): The huge-but-delicate, clear yellow, four-petaled blossoms of Ozark sundrop appear to be twisted from tissue paper. They fairly glow in both harsh and soft light. The plant has a relaxed spreading form, red stems, and waxy, long, narrow leaves. It flowers for most of the summer. The four-winged papery seedpods are also interesting and are so huge that they don't appear to come from the same plant.

Give Ozark sundrop any well-drained soil. It may rot if its roots stay too wet, so let the soil dry out between waterings.

Ozark sundrop is drought tolerant with an occasional deep soaking, but it doesn't like heat combined with humidity. The blooms continue without regular deadheading, making it a good plant for the lazy gardener. Cut it back to the ground annually in winter, and this plant asks for nothing more. It's hardy to –30° F (–34° C).

✔ **Wild sweet William** (*Phlox carolina*): Not as well-known as its cousin, garden phlox, wild sweet William phlox (or spotted phlox) is more adaptable and mildew-resistant. It produces plump clusters of delicate, five-petaled blooms for many weeks. Strong, upright stems support whorls of glossy, narrow leaves. 'Alpha' is rose with a dark eye. 'Miss Lingard' is clear white. Among the hybrids, 'Alpha' is rose with a dark eye, and 'Omega' is palest pink with a violet eye. All are highly fragrant and make good cut flowers.

Plant wild sweet William in well-drained, moist, humus-amended soil. Spotted phlox is the best tall phlox for hot, humid climates, but it's also very cold-hardy. Deadhead finished flowers for reblooming (see Chapter 10) and fertilize and water regularly. Seedlings that pop up here and there usually revert to the mauve pink of the unimproved form. Phlox likes afternoon shade in hot, dry climates and full sun elsewhere. It's hardy to –40° F (–40° C).

✔ **Obedient plant** (*Physostegia virginiana*): As its name implies, obedient plant is generally easy to grow — although I have killed a few by letting them get too dry. When it's happy, obedient plant forms expanding colonies of upright stems and lance-shaped fresh green leaves. Its tubular flowers are tightly arranged in rows at sharp right angles to one another. 'Vivid' is a dwarf deep pink. 'Summer Snow' is white. 'Variegata' is pink with white leaf margins.

Obedient plant can spread very quickly in rich soil, so you may need to divide it annually to control its expansion. Most sources recommend acidic soil, but my plants are perfectly fine in highly alkaline clay. Fertilize and water it regularly. Drier soil is acceptable with afternoon shade. The blooms persist for several weeks and are an outstanding cut flower. The seedheads are attractive in winter. Obedient plant is hardy to –40° F (–40° C).

✔ **Strawberry cinquefoil** (*Potentilla nepalensis* 'Miss Willmott'): The dark green, heavily textured, five-part leaflets of strawberry cinquefoil are arranged in a casually sprawling form. Cheerful pink flowers with dark centers are borne in loose clusters at the ends of arching stems for most of the summer. Strawberry cinquefoil likes cool nights and dislikes heat combined with humidity. The name strawberry cinquefoil refers to the strawberry-like foliage.

Cut back leggy stems by half to keep the plant compact. This plant needs well-drained but not overly fertile soil, so let it dry out between waterings. Strawberry cinquefoil is intolerant of wet soil in winter and may be short-lived. In really hot climates, provide afternoon shade. It's hardy to –20° F (–29° C).

✔ **Orange coneflower** (*Rudbeckia fulgida sullivantii*): Easy, cheerful, uncomplaining, and long-blooming from mid-summer through the first frost, coneflowers grow happily almost anywhere. Their large golden daisies are accented with flat, dark brown center disks. Standing straight and upright, they form dense colonies 2 feet (60 cm) tall and feature handsome dark green foliage. *Rudbeckia fulgida* 'Goldstrum' is a popular variety developed in Germany.

Orange coneflower is not particular about climate, soil, or moisture, but it performs best in fertile soil with ample moisture and full sun. Deadhead the spent blooms until late in the season and leave the last wave of flowers to dry on the stalks for winter interest. The flowers are good for cutting. If you grow them in partial shade, the plants lose their compact form and get a bit leggy. They're hardy to –40° F (–40° C).

A cousin of the orange coneflower, three-lobed cone-flower (*Rudbeckia triloba*) is short-lived but self-sows with abandon, so its progeny pop up here and there. This is a big plant with masses of tiny, golden, black-eyed daisies. Hardy from the harsh winter to hot, humid climates, this plant grows in sun or partial shade and prefers some moisture.

✔ **Pincushion flower** (*Scabiosa caucasica*): The handful of perennials with pincushion-style blossoms are especially valuable for the contrast they provide against other, more familiar flower shapes. With pincushion flowers, a fluffy center tuft is surrounded by a lacy, ruffled row of petals. The flowerheads are held gracefully on long stems and come in many shades of blue, lavender, pink, and white. The leaves are long, narrow, and pointed.

Pincushion flowers are easy to grow in well-drained, fertile soil with regular watering. They prefer alkaline conditions and benefit from added lime where soil pH is low (see Chapter 6). The plants bloom for months if you regularly deadhead them (see Chapter 10). They prefer climates with cool summer nights. Winter wet can be fatal; use a loose winter mulch to protect crowns in really cold regions. These flowers are hardy to –50° F (–46° C).

A relative of *Scabiosa caucasica*, *Scabiosa columbaria* 'Butterfly Blue' and 'Pink Mist' are dwarf plants that bloom all summer and attract butterflies. *Scabiosa ochroleuca* has the softest butter-yellow flowers and is extremely vigorous and drought tolerant.

✔ **Goldenrod** (*Solidago rugosa* 'Fireworks'): The attention-grabbing, golden yellow starburst flowers of goldenrod look very much like exploding sky rockets. The individual flowers are small, but their numbers make up for their size, forming graceful plumes over compact clumps of red-tinged foliage. The flowers are good for cutting or drying and are attractive to butterflies. They bloom for several weeks. In spite of the rumors you may have heard, goldenrod does not cause hay fever.

Dwarf goldenrod (*Solidago glomerata* 'Golden Baby') is 2 to 2½ feet (60 to 75 cm) tall, golden yellow, and quite drought tolerant.

Goldenrod is native to the southeastern U.S. and appreciates an open site with fairly fertile soil and plenty of moisture. It slowly expands into a good-sized clump. You can leave the flowers to dry on the plant late in the season for fall texture — cut them off after snow has smashed down the stems. Goldenrod is hardy to –30° F (–34° C).

✔ **Lamb's ears** (*Stachys byzantina*): Lamb's ears is everyone's favorite silver-foliage perennial. The leaves are as soft as flannel and invite touching. In fact, few people can resist feeling the lamb's ears. The plant grows in loose rosettes that expand outward into mats. The flower stalks are as heavily felted as the leaves. The flowers, a delicate purplish pink, are a good choice for cut flowers — fresh or dried. 'Silver Carpet' is a non-flowering variety for those who don't want the flower.

Lamb's ears likes any fairly well-drained soil, moist or dry, but may rot in hot, humid climates. 'Helen von Stein' is a large-leafed form that is less likely to melt down. These plants are hardy to –30° F (–34° C).

If the plants die out in the center, dig up the whole mat and replant a few pieces. It spreads quickly and can be a bit of a nuisance, but (I think) a pleasant one. I'm always digging up plants that are busily consuming paths and putting them back where I want them to be.

✔ **Rose verbena** (*Verbena canadensis*): A vigorous and freely-blooming plant, rose verbena forms relaxed, spreading clumps. Its stems root wherever they touch the ground. The bright pink flowers form rounded clusters that last all summer; the foliage is crisp and evergreen. Many color variations exist — you can find lilac, red, white, and rose. 'Homestead Purple' is an outstanding bright purple.

Rose verbena's winter hardiness is variable, and not one variety has ever survived a winter in my Colorado garden. But I replant it every year, give it a winter mulch, and cross my fingers. Plant it in any well-drained soil; rose verbena rots if it's kept too wet, but it's quite drought tolerant. Cut the stems in half if they get too tall and leggy. This plant attracts butterflies and is hardy to –20° F (–29° C).

✔ **Spiked speedwell** (*Veronica spicata*): Hard to beat for late summer color, speedwell comes into its own when most of the perennial garden is having a heat-induced snooze. For nearly two months, speedwell produces dense spires of deep blue flowers over tight mats of shiny green or soft gray leaves, depending on variety. 'Minuet' is pink with silvery foliage. 'Blue Charm' is a good lavender blue. 'Red Fox' is dark rose.

Speedwell likes any well-drained soil with regular waterings. Poor drainage combined with hot, humid weather is a certain killer. To keep the plants compact, don't over-fertilize. Its clumps increase slowly, never invasively. 'Goodness Grows' tolerates hot, humid climates better than most. Remove the spent flowers for continued blossoming. Speedwell are hardy to –30° F (–34° C).

✔ **Prairie zinnia** (*Zinnia grandiflora*): Most folks know the popular annual zinnias, but gardeners in arid regions have become better acquainted with a charming little wildflower cousin, the prairie zinnia, which brings a splash of bright yellow to the dry-climate garden. Low mounds of tiny, narrow foliage spread to create solid colonies. The flowers are golden yellow, sometimes with red centers, and dry to a papery texture.

Prairie zinnia can be difficult to transplant. You must water it whenever the soil dries out until the plants are growing strongly. Give it well-drained, infertile soil in arid and semiarid regions. Individual plants are long-lived and slow to spread. Prairie zinnia can survive on desert rainfall, but the plants grow more strongly with a good soaking once or twice a month. Late to break dormancy in spring, prairie zinnia is hardy to –30° F (–34° C).

Chapter 5

Made for Shade

. . . .

In This Chapter

▶ Increasing your odds for a successful shade garden

▶ Designing a shady bed

▶ Extending the bloom season

▶ Perusing perennials for your shady spots

. . . .

*I*f you garden in shade, you may be disappointed on your first trip to your local garden center to find that the number of shade-loving plants is considerably smaller than the selection of perennials for sunny gardens. The list in this chapter reflects this reality as well. But don't despair. Take a closer look, and you discover that most of the sun-loving flowers I list in Chapter 4 can also handle at least partial or dappled shade. These plants may not flower as freely in the shade as they would in full sunlight, but the large majority of them can cope with some shade.

If you're dealing with extremes — for example, very dense shade with either soggy wet or very dry soils — the number of adapted perennials you can choose from is quite limited. If at all possible, give serious thought to moving your flower bed to a more suitable place. Alternatively, you may choose to thin out a few trees to bring in more light or to install drainage tiles or a watering system. If none of these solutions appeals to you, just enjoy the selection of perennials that can tolerate such extremes — and be sure to give them lots of encouragement and praise for their adaptability.

Making Perennials at Home in the Shade

A recurring theme among shade-loving perennials is a woodland origin. Most perennials that do well in the shade appreciate the typical conditions found in the forest.

- ✓ Give them a loose, porous soil, deeply dug, with plenty of added humus to get them off to a strong start. (See Chapter 6 for more on soils.)

- ✓ After planting, re-create the leaf litter found on the forest floor by spreading 2 to 3 inches (5 to 8 cm) of a light, airy, organic mulch, such as pine needles, between the plants. (Turn to Chapter 11 for tips on mulch.)

- ✓ When experimenting with flowers that normally fancy more abundant sunlight, give each plant plenty of elbow room so that it can take full advantage of whatever light reaches it. Spacing plants more widely in shade also creates better air circulation, which helps prevent foliage diseases.

You can easily measure whether a particular perennial is adapting to its shady environment by watching its performance. When a flower fails to bloom or starts to look pretty darn pathetic — with anemic, yellowing leaves on spindly, weak, and sprawling stems — it's time to admit defeat. Put the poor thing up for adoption to a sunnier home and try another plant.

On the other hand, when a shade plant is getting too much sunlight, it also lets you know that it's unhappy. The leaves generally bleach out and become papery thin, or they may actually sunburn and develop scorched patches and brown margins. Plants are every bit as efficient at showing their displeasure as my pet spaniel — after you learn to read their signals.

Planning a Flower Bed in the Shade

Designing a shade garden is no more complicated than designing any other flowerbed. As always, the key to successful gardening is choosing plants that are compatible with your site or modifying the site enough to accommodate the flowers that you're bound and determined to grow.

For a shady location, you can either plant shade-lovers or cut down the trees that are blocking the sun. Planting shade-lovers is much less work. Besides, if the shade is cast by a structure, you don't have the second option — unless your neighbors agree to knock over their house or garage so that you can have a nice, sunny garden.

In some respects, designing for shade is simpler and more satisfying than designing for sun because the focus on flowers is automatically diminished. Flower color is only one part of putting together an outstanding garden. Foliage shape, color, and texture are all equally essential elements. Shady perennials win hands-down over their sunny counterparts in this respect. Where light is low, catching sunlight becomes more important than conserving moisture loss through evaporation. The result is plants (such as hostas and heartleaf bergenia) with massive leaves. Add a few ferns, and you certainly don't need to worry about texture.

If you close your eyes and imagine a forest glen, you probably picture lush green. But your woodland garden doesn't have to be endlessly green. You can add extra sparkle by choosing varied foliage colors. Green hostas are pretty, but you can also select varieties with leaves of golden, glowing yellow, and elegant blue. Other varieties of hostas come in a seemingly limitless spectrum of two-tones with yellow, cream, or white markings. Play off the dull green of perennial forget-me-nots against the shine of heart-leaf bergenia. Throw in a splash of purple with some of the vibrant coral bells. Now that's a flower bed!

Getting More Blooms with Less Sun

To be fair, I must admit that the shaded garden doesn't flower as freely as the flower bed in full sun. Most of the perennials in this chapter bloom in spring and then are unobtrusive for the rest of the year.

To add flower appeal to your shady garden, leave space among the perennials for a few annuals to keep the flowering season going longer. Ageratums, browallias, fuchsias, tuberous begonias, coleus, impatiens, baby-blue-eyes, cinerarias, Canterbury bells, monkey flowers, flowering tobacco, and wishbone flowers all do well in shade. Where tree roots interfere with planting annuals, grow them in pots and set them beneath the tree. Or hang baskets of annuals from lower limbs for another splash of color.

Many bulbs have woodland ancestors and do well in the shade, giving you the opportunity to add more color. If your garden is shaded by deciduous trees and has unobstructed sunlight during the winter months, you can likely grow any of the early sun-loving spring bulbs such as tulips, daffodils, and crocuses. These flowers bloom before the trees don their spring leaves.

Other spring-blooming bulbs prefer some shade. Tuck any of these bulbs here and there in between the other flowers:

- Windflowers (*Anemone blanda*)
- Camass (*Camassia*)
- Glory-of-the-snow (*Chionodoxa*)
- Spanish bluebells (*Endymion hispanicus*)
- Winter aconites (*Eranthis hyemalis*)
- Dog-toothed violets (*Erythronium dens-canis*)
- Snowflakes (*Leucojum*)
- Grape hyacinths (*Muscari*)
- Squill (*Scilla*)

 For additional summer foliage color, pop in a few fancy-leafed caladiums or coleus. They come in a huge number of bright — even flamboyant — colors. Although both caladiums and coleus have insignificant blossoms, their foliage is so extravagant that you probably won't miss the flowers.

Perennials Made for the Shade

The following list is just a handful of the hundreds of true shade-loving perennials in circulation. Some of these plants absolutely insist on shade. Others don't mind direct sunlight in varying degrees, depending on your climate and light intensity. You can plant many of them in full sun if you live in a region where summers are generally cool and overcast.

- **Lady's mantle** (*Alchemilla mollis*): Lady's mantle is perfectly content in full sun in cloudy, overcast climates, but its leaves get badly scorched by intense sunlight. Called lady's mantle because each leaf resembles a pleated cape, this is a luxuriant plant with foliage every bit as attractive as the flowers. The flowers, a froth of chartreuse yellow, bloom from spring through most of the summer and are outstanding when cut. This plant can withstand average wintertime lows to −30° F (−34° C).

  Lady's mantle thrives in woodland conditions with moist but not sopping wet soil. It's more tolerant of dry soil in shade than in sun. This plant can be quite invasive, spreading into large patches and also seeding some distance away. Remove spent flowers to slow down spreading. Lady's mantle does best in regions with cool overnight temperatures and can withstand extreme winter cold, but it isn't tolerant of heat combined with humidity in subtropical regions.

- **Japanese painted fern** (*Athyrium niponicum* 'Pictum'): Ferns are synonymous with shade. But if you automatically picture green foliage when you think ferns, this one comes as a complete surprise. The fronds are grayish green overlaid with silver. To add more complexity to this color combination, the mid-ribs are burgundy red. The foliage is heavily cut and filigreed for a delicate and graceful texture.

  This fern is more rugged than its appearance suggests; it grows easily in well-drained, humus-enriched soil in either shade or partial shade. Early to emerge in spring, the Japanese painted fern goes dormant if you allow it to get too dry during the growing season. Protect and preserve moisture with several inches of light organic mulch. It sends up new fronds throughout the summer, but its deciduous fronds die back to the ground in winter. This plant is a good choice for any climate except subtropical — it's hardy to −40° F (−40° C).

- **Pigsqueak** (*Bergenia cordifolia*): You probably haven't heard the name pigsqueak unless you live in Colorado. This plant is usually called by its botanical name, *bergenia,* but pigsqueak is more memorable and certainly more descriptive. If you pinch a leaf in your moistened fingertips, you can produce a very pig-like squeal (and liven up those dull parties). Pigsqueak has large, thick, glossy leaves in open rosettes and pink flower spikes very early in the spring.

This plant's evergreen foliage turns red during wintertime in mild climates. In climates with colder winters, pigsqueak is deciduous — or ratty enough that you wish the foliage would take a winter vacation. Although pigsqueak tolerates a full sun position in cloudy, cool regions, it prefers shade everywhere else. Any soil is fine, but too much fertilizing makes this plant floppy. It's fairly drought tolerant in dry shade. Slugs can do a great deal of damage to this plant (see Chapter 12 for tips on dealing with these slimy critters). Pigsqueak is hardy to –40° F (–40° C).

✔ **Bleeding heart** (*Dicentra hybrids*): The hybrid bleeding hearts are unbeatable. They are the ideal perennial — blooming for six months, long-lived, adaptable, easy-care, and possessing beautiful foliage. Clusters of charming, locket-shaped flowers hang over deeply cut, ferny foliage. 'Luxuriant' is deep pink, 'Snowdrift' is white, and 'Bountiful' is rosy red. All are hardy to –40° F (–40° C).

All parts of bleeding hearts, if eaten, are toxic to both you and your pets. The roots contain the largest concentration of poison, so be especially careful when these plants are out of the ground.

Bleeding hearts can be placed in full sun in cool climates, but they prefer shade anywhere else. They want a humus-enriched, moisture-retentive but not wet soil. But because I don't have such a site, mine have to make do in heavy clay under a pine tree. They don't seem to object. The clumps expand slowly and are never invasive. This plant is not a good choice for hot, humid subtropical gardens.

✔ **Lenten rose** (*Helleborus orientalis*): If you don't already have a shady spot on your property, Lenten roses are enough of an incentive to plant a tree. Dramatic and elegant, they are among the first non-bulb flowers to bloom in the spring. The foliage is handsome, glossy, and evergreen except in the coldest winters. The flowers are open bells of cream to soft rose, often with purple freckles and a touch of the palest green.

Lenten roses are long-lived and easy to grow in any climate with wintertime lows above –30° F (–34° C). The clumps mature and increase very slowly, so buy large plants, or you may wait several years to see these lovely flowers for the first time. They like plenty of moisture and soil enriched with organic matter but also tolerate dry shade well in my garden. Some years the foliage and first flowers are zapped by cold temperatures. Cut them off, and the plants readily bounce back. Mulch plants heavily to preserve soil moisture.

✔ **Coral bells** (*Heuchera sanguinea*): Amazing things are being done to your grandmother's coral bells. They are currently undergoing extensive selection and hybridization. Every year a few more of these beauties hit the market. Varieties with attractive flowers come in shades of red, pink, coral, and white. The types chosen for outstanding foliage usually don't offer much in the flower department, but what an amazing array of leaf colors! Speckled and splashed, washed in silver, deep purples, and subtle reds — each more fetching than the last.

Plant coral bells in a woodland-type soil, fertilize with plenty of humus, and provide consistent moisture. Full sun works in cloudy climates, but not where sunlight is truly intense. This plant is intolerant of wet soil in winter, so provide good drainage. Use an organic mulch year round and cover with pine boughs or other lightweight winter protection in bitterly cold regions. The foliage is evergreen in mild climates.

Coral bells are best in cool climates (withstanding wintertime lows to –40° F [–40° C]) but are also quite comfortable in dry heat. Breeding for hot, humid climates is a current focus, so expect more of these coming soon.

✔ **Virginia bluebells** (*Mertensia virginica*): Wherever you grow hostas or ferns, you must throw in a few Virginia bluebells. They are easy-care, long-lived wildflowers that put up with neglect and mistreatment without complaint and are hardy to –40° F (–40° C). The leaves, green with purple tints, emerge in late winter or early spring. The flowers are nodding clusters of tubular bells, opening pink and aging to lavender blue.

Bluebells go dormant with the beginning of hot weather, so always place them where other perennials hide their death throes. After the yellowing foliage starts to brown, cut it off — the only care these low-maintenance flowers ever need. They do best in fertile, moist soil, especially in spring when they're just coming out of dormancy. The plants slowly spread to fill all the barren spaces in the shade garden.

✔ **Jacob's ladder** (*Polemonium caeruleum*): This plant features loose clusters of five-petaled, soft blue flowers on spikes above ladder-shaped leaflets. The blossoms are ornamented with prominent yellow stamens. Jacob's ladder is long-blooming, especially if faded flower spikes are removed. It's also available in a white form. 'Apricot Delight' is lavender with apricot centers. *Polemonium reptans* 'Blue Pearl' is bright blue.

Unfortunately, this plant is not adapted to hot, humid climates. Jacob's ladder is hardy to –50° F (–45° C), but if you live in a subtropical climate, this plant isn't a good choice for you. Where nights are cool and dry, it's dependable and easy to grow. My plants struggled for years until I moved them to a shaded spot within a few feet of a rock wall base in heavy clay soil. They do well in full sun only in cooler, cloudy climates. For best results, water regularly.

✔ **Foam flower** (*Tiarella cordifolia*): A relative unknown, foam flower has suddenly become increasingly popular as hybridizers play around with leaf shape and color and flower color. The original plant has toothed, heart-shaped leaves with burgundy veining and attractive, bronze red fall color. The flowers are delicate and starry. New varieties feature deeply cut, ruffled, and brightly-colored foliage and fragrant pink, coral, or white flowers.

The foliage is evergreen in mild areas. These flowers are best in cool shade, but they can stand heat as long as they are kept well-watered. Amend the soil with plenty of organic matter and plant in partial to full shade. Use an organic mulch to keep the soil cool and moist. Water before the soil dries out completely. Although foam flower isn't adapted to the muggiest subtropical regions, it is fast-growing and quickly forms good-sized colonies elsewhere. Foam flower can withstand average wintertime lows of –40° F (–40° C).

Chapter 6

The Dirt on Dirt

In This Chapter

▷ Becoming acquainted with your soil

▷ Solving soil chemical problems

▷ Preparing good soil

*O*ther mortals dream of wealth, fame, and riches, but gardeners are a different sort. What they yearn for is the elusive perfect soil. Good soil makes all the difference between a garden that prospers and one that struggles and sulks. When you begin to recognize soil as a living, breathing, and evolving entity that needs as much monitoring and care as the flowers themselves, you've cracked the code to successful gardening.

The ideal soil for most perennials is deep and porous, neither holding too much water nor drying out too quickly. Perennials also prefer soils rich in plant nutrients and *humus* — decomposed organic matter.

Unlike vegetable gardens, where gardeners recharge the soil between crops, flower beds are more permanent features. Initially digging fertilizer and such into the ground to correct deficiencies in your soil (a procedure called *amending* soil) is hard work, but all your sweat and blisters are repaid many times over. If you prepare and maintain a flower bed correctly, you may never need to dig it again.

Getting to Know Your Soil

Soil is a mixture of decaying organic matter, air, water, living organisms, and various types of weathered rock. Factors such as the bedrock composition, climate, and topography unique to each area can cause soil ingredients to vary dramatically from one region to the next.

Testing texture

A soil's *texture* (that is, its fineness or coarseness) has nothing to do with organic-matter or nutrient makeup. Soil texture is defined by its relative volume of three types of mineral particles:

- ✔ **Sand:** The stuff of beaches and sandboxes, sand is coarse and gritty. It drains well, but it dries out too quickly for most perennials. Sandy soil doesn't compact and is easy to cultivate, but nutrients wash out of it too readily.

- ✔ **Silt:** Silt is similar to sand, but the individual particles are much smaller. When silt is dry, it feels like flour. Silt holds water longer than sand, but not as tightly as clay.

- ✔ **Clay:** Clay is so fine that each particle can be seen only with an electron microscope. Clay soils are sticky to the touch and drain slowly. Some clays liquefy when wet and then dry to the consistency of concrete. Clay cakes on shoes and tools. It's high in nutrients, but these nutrients often occur in forms unavailable to plants.

Fortunately, few soils are composed of only one of these mineral particle types — most soils are a combination of all three.

When the mineral particles occur in ideal proportions, the soil is called *loam*. Loam contains 10 to 20 percent clay, 25 to 70 percent silt, and 20 to 60 percent sand. Very few gardeners get loam. You probably have to make do with soil that contains too high a percentage of either sand or clay for the perennials you plan to grow. Determining your soil's texture is critical because each type has distinct characteristics and management requirements. You may also find that you have several types of soil. Probably more than one truck load of fill dirt was used to contour your property, and each load may have originated from many different sources.

You can get a fairly accurate measure of your soil's texture by using one or both of the following simple tests. Get ready to re-live your seventh grade science class.

The feel test

To conduct the feel test, grab a fistful of moist — not squishy wet — soil and squeeze it into a ball. Examine the results:

- ✔ Sand doesn't hold together very well and feels gritty and coarse.

- ✔ Silt can hold a shape fairly well and feels smooth but not sticky. If you roll silt between your palms, it forms a fat clump but doesn't hold a rope shape.

- ✔ Clay feels slippery, and you can roll it between the palms of your hands into an elongated rope shape.

If your handful of soil holds its shape briefly and then slowly crumbles apart to look like chocolate cake crumbs, congratulations! You've won the soil lottery! You have loam or a soil with a large percentage of organic matter. Either soil is perfect for a wide range of perennials.

The jar test

The jar test is a low-tech version of the soil lab's texture test, one that you can do at home. It tells you the basic character of your soil — whether your soil is predominantly sand, silt, or clay.

1. **Add 1 inch (2.5 cm) of dry soil to a quart jar.**

   Mayonnaise and peanut butter jars do nicely.

2. **Fill the jar two-thirds full of water.**

3. **Add one teaspoon of non-sudsing detergent or water softener.**

4. **Screw on the lid and shake the jar vigorously.**

5. **Set the jar where it can be left completely undisturbed for at least three days.**

6. **After three days, measure each layer that settles out.**

   The layers are quite distinct, as shown in Figure 6-1.

7. **Multiply the depth of each layer by 100 and then divide each result by the total depth of all three layers.**

The number that you calculate is the percentage of each particle type. Sand is the heaviest and forms the bottom layer. Silt forms the middle layer, and clay is on top. (Some clay particles are so light that they float in suspension indefinitely.)

Water

Clay

Silt

Sand

Figure 6-1: The jar test in action.

Complete soil testing

For a more accurate, complete soil test, contact your state's cooperative extension service, usually located at the state agricultural college or a private laboratory. A soil test isn't essential unless you're experiencing problems or you suspect that your soil is high in salt, but knowing the availability of the various soil nutrients can guide you to more efficient fertilizer use. You don't need to add elements that the soil test indicates already exist in your soil in sufficient quantities. The soil test results include recommendations for improving the soil, and that advice can be very helpful for the new gardener.

Soil tests do have their limitations. The sample you send to the lab is an average of soils collected throughout the garden. The smaller the garden, the more likely the sample is representative of the conditions there. Usually one test is all you need. Inexpensive home tests enable you to monitor soil pH, as well as nitrogen, phosphorus, and potassium levels routinely thereafter.

Desperately seeking structure

Soil structure is determined by the way the individual particles of sand, silt, and clay clump together. When a soil has
good structure, it includes plenty of space for air and water.
The earth under your feet is not as solid as your senses tell
you. Healthy soil contains approximately 50 percent solids
(mineral particles and organic matter), 25 percent water, and
25 percent air. Many physical forces (including root expansion
in the soils, wet and dry cycles, freezing and thawing, and
earthworm activity) push these solids together.

The glue that cements the lumps of soil together may be clay
particles or chemical substances. One glue that you can easily
add yourself is organic matter. Picture a bowl of dry popcorn
and peanuts. Now imagine adding sticky syrup. If you pour the
syrup over the top without stirring, a solid mass forms — a
popcorn-peanut brick. But when you mix all the ingredients
together, clumps form instead, and you end up with caramel
corn. In much the same way, digging organic matter into light
soils creates crumbs and openings (pores) that give plant
roots, air, water, and nutrients easy access into and through
the soil.

Organic matter is the cure to almost every soil problem you
encounter. Adding it to sandy soil increases the soil's capacity
to hold water and nutrients. Organic matter loosens clay and
creates pockets for air and water. Organic matter also nur-
tures the populations of microorganisms, insects, and worms
that make their home in the soil. They, in turn, break the
organic matter down into a form of nutrients that the plant
roots can absorb.

Fertile soil contains a minimum of 5 percent decaying organic
matter, but soil can hardly contain too much of this material if
you compost and age the organic matter a while before you
add it to the garden.

You damage soil structure by working the soil when it's wet or
by compacting it (wet or dry) with machinery or foot traffic.
To demonstrate compacted soil, take a shovel full of damp
soil and fluff it up by turning it several times and breaking
apart large clods. Now pile this soil onto a flat surface and
step on it. It flattens considerably — you've just crushed out
most of the pore spaces and compacted the soil.

Looking at layers

Soils occur in three separate layers, but only the top two layers, topsoil and subsoil, concern the gardener. You can easily observe the three layers in road cuts or excavation sites.

✔ **Topsoil:** The fertile band of soil on the surface, where organic matter accumulates and most of the soil organisms and plant roots reside, is called topsoil. This layer is usually 4 to 6 inches (10 to 15 cm) thick but is sometimes much deeper. Topsoil is deepest in prairies and meadows with moderate rainfall and is more shallow on slopes, in forests, and in areas with dry climates. In semiarid regions, topsoil is only one or two inches deep.

When building a new residence, arrange for the contractor to save your topsoil and put it back when construction is complete. This valuable resource is worth the extra cost and work you put into preserving it.

✔ **Subsoil:** The layer under the topsoil, subsoil can be up to several feet (about a meter) deep. Subsoil stores water and nutrients that have rinsed through the topsoil from above. Usually low in organic matter and free of weed seeds, subsoil often has a finer texture because clay particles filter down and collect at this level. Subsoil is denser and more compacted than topsoil. The fill around a new house is often subsoil from the site's excavation.

✔ **Bottomsoil:** The bottom layer of soil is made up of decomposed bedrock. The only things you find growing in bottomsoil are tree roots.

Soil Chemistry Simplified

Soil acidity or alkalinity is expressed as *pH* on a scale of 1 to 14. The higher the pH, the greater the alkalinity; the lower the pH, the greater the acidity. A pH of 7.0 is neutral. For comparison purposes, the pH of grapefruit is 3.0 and the pH of milk of magnesia is 10. The optimum pH for most perennials is 6.5 to 7.5, though all but the most sensitive can tolerate a pH of 5.5 to 8.3 without developing problems. Some types of plants can grow at the edge of the 3.5 to 10 range, but only a limited number of plants can flourish where the soil pH is so extreme.

In pine and oak forests and in regions where rainfall exceeds 25 inches (60 cm) annually, soil tends to be acidic. Where rainfall is less than 25 inches annually, most soils are alkaline or close to neutral. But the only way to be certain is to test your soil. Kits that use litmus paper or a test tube are easy to use and inexpensive. They can be purchased at garden centers or hardware stores. Just follow the label instructions carefully.

Neutralizing very acidic soil

Where soil pH measures below 5.5, the selection of perennials that you can grow is severely restricted. Many perennials fail at this pH. Some essential nutrients become unavailable to the plant; others can rise to toxic levels. If your soil pH is below 5.5, you have two options:

 ✔ Choose perennials that are adapted to acidic soil (see Table 6-1 for a few perennials that don't mind acidic soil).

 ✔ Raise the pH by adding lime.

Lime is available as agricultural lime, ground limestone, calcium carbonate, or dolomite limestone. Check with your state's cooperative extension service for recommendations on which type is best for your local conditions, and follow their recommended application rates.

Don't attempt to raise the pH more than one point in a single season. Make it a gradual process for better results. Work the lime into the top 6 to 8 inches (15 to 20 cm) of the soil several months before planting, and don't add fertilizer within one month of adding lime. In cold weather, affecting a change can take as long as six months. In warm weather, three months is usually sufficient. Heavy, clay soils require more lime than light, sandy soils. Test the pH levels once or twice a season to monitor changes after adding lime.

Table 6-1	Perennials for Acidic Soil	
Common Name	**Botanical Name**	**Sun Requirements**
Butterfly flower	Asclepias tuberosa	Sun
Thousand-flowered aster	Boltonia asteroides	Partial shade/sun
Dutchman's breeches	Dicentra cucullaria	Shade/partial shade
Japanese iris	Iris ensata	Partial shade/sun
Lupine	Lupinus Russell Hybrids	Partial shade/sun
Himalayan blue poppy	Meconopsis betonicifolia	Partial shade/sun
Virginia bluebells	Mertensia virginica	Shade/partial shade
Allegheny monkey flower	Mimulus ringens	Partial shade
Cinnamon fern	Osmunda cinnamomea	Shade/sun
Primrose	Primula auricula	Partial shade

Coping with alkaline soils

Soils with a pH higher than 8.3 can limit the availability of phosphorus, iron, zinc, and magnesium. An irony with Colorado's soils is that, although their bright red color is caused by an abundance of iron in the soil, the iron is in a form that's unavailable to plants. Plants growing in this iron-rich soil often suffer from iron deficiency.

Acid-loving perennials are the least tolerant of high pH and become yellowed and stunted (a condition called *chlorosis*) due to nutrient shortages. Because these soils generally occur in arid and semiarid regions, they also tend to be low in organic matter and high in salts.

Lowering pH is more difficult than raising it, but you can do a few things to make alkaline soil more acidic. You can add peat moss, ground needles, or oak leaves and add acidifying minerals such as sulfur, ferrous sulfate, and ammonium sulfate. Follow the manufacturer's recommended amounts. Regular irrigation also eventually reduces pH unless the water is high in soluble salts.

Where pH is high and water isn't plentiful, prepare only one flower bed for your favorite perennials that demand altered soil. Then plan the rest of the garden around the wide selection of native and adapted flowers that accept the existing conditions. Keep in mind that perennials that originate in acidic soils may also be intolerant of the strong sunlight and the low humidity that are typical of climates where alkaline soils are common. In this case, locate the flower bed where it can enjoy the morning sun and afternoon shade.

Making the Bed

Prepare the soil several months before you anticipate planting if you can. This schedule gives a new bed time to settle down and microorganisms a chance to work on the soil amendments and sort out any imbalances. In cold climates, plan to do soil preparation in the fall in order to plant the following spring. Or reverse this schedule where summers are hot and winters are mild: Get the bed ready in spring or early summer for fall planting.

Mark the outlines of the flowerbed according to your plan. Tie string between two stakes to mark straight lines and lay out flexible garden hose to define the curves. (Leave the hose out in the sun for a while if it is stiff or kinky. Rubber hoses are more flexible than plastic.) Play around with the dimensions and lines until you create a pleasing shape.

Clearing the site

Mow or use a power weed whacker to cut down any existing lawn or weeds. Be sure that you remove all the seedheads. For shrubs that need to be disposed of, cut off the tops and dig out the stumps and as many large roots as possible. Desirable shrubs can be carefully dug out and transplanted or left in place if your design calls for them. If left in the bed, leave as many roots undisturbed as practical. You can safely cut away those that are outside an imaginary circle on the ground that is as wide as the widest part of the top of the shrub.

Kill weeds or sod with one of the following methods:

- ✔ **Herbicides:** Use a product containing glyphosate according to the directions on the label. Persistent weeds may need multiple treatments.

- ✔ **Smothering with newspapers:** Spread a ¼-inch thickness of newspapers over the bed, overlapping the edges generously. Cover the newspapers with 6 inches of an organic mulch that decays rapidly. Straw or hay are good choices. Leave the newspaper in place for one growing season. If your soil is decent to begin with, you can plant right through the mulch and paper. If it isn't, dig the newspaper and mulch in together as a soil amendment.

- ✔ **Solarization:** Solarization is the process of sterilizing the soil with sunlight and the heat it generates. This process is especially useful where soil-borne diseases or pests are a problem. Animals simply leave, and most of the weeds and microorganisms (good and bad) are killed. After solarization, you need to reintroduce microorganisms by mixing compost or organic matter into the soil. (See the sidebar, "Solar power," for step-by-step instructions on solarizing your flower bed.)

To remove the dead sod, use a rented mechanical sod stripper or a spade. Better yet, till the sod right into the soil — sod is a great source of organic matter and nutrients. Left on the ground, the dead roots, leaves, and thatch create a well-amended layer 6 to 8 inches (15 to 21 cm) deep. Most important, you don't have to haul the heavy sod off to the compost pile to dispose of it.

Where the soil underneath is reasonably well-drained, you can save even more labor by planting right through the dead sod without rototilling. For each plant, cut out a circle of sod twice as large as the circumference of the plant container, or twice as wide as the root ball (if transplanting). Proceed by following the instructions for planting in Chapter 7.

Solar power

Because the process of solarization relies on the sun's heat, you must solarize in warm weather. To solarize your soil, follow these steps:

1. **Loosen soil with a rototiller or a shovel.**

2. **Water the area well.**

3. **Cover the bed with clear plastic sheeting.**

   Clear plastic sheeting is available in garden centers and hardware stores.

4. **Pin the plastic in place with landscape pins or pieces of wire and seal the edges with soil or boards.**

5. **Leave the plastic in place for several weeks or over the summer before proceeding.**

After solarizing your soil, be sure to import useful microorganisms back into the sterilized soil by digging in several inches of compost.

Choosing a soil amendment

You can't add too much organic material to your soil — just be sure that you use material that is well aged or composted. Use a minimum of one-third volume of organic material to one volume of soil to be amended. For example, dig at least 2 inches (5 cm) of organic matter into 6 inches (15 cm) of soil. Perfect soil, although rare, does exist occasionally. If you're one of the lucky ones and are starting out with a crumbly, rich loam, you have the option of skipping the whole process of soil amending if you want (although adding 2 to 3 inches (5 to 8 cm) of compost never hurts, especially if you plan to grow a large variety of perennials in close quarters). Where compaction is the only problem of an otherwise good soil, fluffing it up with a rototiller or hand digging may be all you need to do to restore good structure and prepare the bed for planting.

A valid alternative to soil preparation is choosing plants that are adapted to your existing soil. Very few soils are so poor that they can't support a satisfactory selection of flowers. But you must be content in this case to let the soil choose the flowers.

The following soil amendments are widely available. Your local garden center or hardware store may not carry all of them, but most of these stores offer a good selection to choose from:

- ✔ **Compost:** Whether your own or commercially developed, compost is the very best soil amendment. It contains beneficial microorganisms and important micronutrients and attracts earthworms that aid soil conditioning.

- ✔ **Cottonseed meal, alfalfa meal, and blood meal:** These amendments are expensive but are good organic sources of nitrogen, which is needed for all plant growth, and organic matter.

- ✔ **Leaf mold:** Ground up, partially decomposed leaves make an excellent soil conditioner. Some communities compost leaves and return the leaf mold to residents.

- ✔ **Manure:** Manure can contain salts, so age it for one year and thoroughly compost it. You can use fresh manure if you don't plant the bed for several months after spreading. One drawback to manure is that it may contain weed seeds.

- ✔ **Peat moss:** Expensive, acidic peat moss is too fine to effectively break up heavy clay. Highly absorbent, peat moss is best used to improve the water-holding capacity of sand. Peat moss is sterile and free of weed seeds and diseases, but it contains no nutrients. Avoid using so-called "mountain peat," which can actually make your soil worse.

- ✔ **Perlite, vermiculite:** These are heat-treated mineral products. They are expensive and are best for seed starting and container-grown perennials.

- ✔ **Calcine:** Certain clay products, such as unscented, natural kitty litter and porous clay, improve the texture of sand or clay.

- ✔ **Pumice, crushed scoria:** These expensive materials can be used to loosen clay soils in small areas or added to soil mixes for container planting. They improve drainage and create pore spaces.

- ✔ **Superphosphate, bone meal:** Phosphorus doesn't move readily through the soil, so adding it during initial soil preparations ensures that it gets down into the root-growing area. Apply at the rate recommended by soil labs or follow the package instructions.

Amending your soil

When your site is clear of weeds, the next step is digging in the soil amendments.

 If the soil is wet, postpone digging until it's only damp. To check the soil, grab a handful and squeeze. If water runs out or clay squishes between your fingers, wait until the soil is drier so that you don't damage the structure of the soil.

Amend the soil by following these steps:

1. **Choose the type of soil amendment you want and arrange for delivery.**

2. **Break up the soil, digging up a shovelful at a time.**

   Turn it over and use the blade of the shovel to chop up large clods. (Singing a chorus of "I want to break free!" helps pass the time!)

3. **Remove any large roots (over an inch [2 cm] or so in diameter), buried construction debris, and large rocks that you find.**

   If you hit bedrock just beneath the surface, you need to rethink the flower bed location or raise the bed.

4. **Spread 2 to 3 inches (5 to 8 cm) of soil amendment on the bed and dig it in thoroughly.**

   Now you can switch to a mechanical tiller or continue by hand. Add organic matter in stages, incorporating each layer into the soil well. Be careful not to till too much; the goal is to mix the materials into the bed but not pulverize the soil.

5. **Scatter commercial fertilizer or minerals on top of the last layer and mix them in.**

When you finish, your soil is light and fluffy. Make sure that you don't walk on it and compact it. Place boards or stepping stones where you need access to the bed. Let the area rest until time to plant or use a temporary cover crop to hold the bare soil in place.

Protecting the soil with a cover crop

A cover crop is any planting that comes up and fills in quickly. It prevents erosion, helps trap rainfall, and shades the ground (which deters remaining weed seeds from sprouting). Legumes such as alfalfa, clover, soybeans, and vetch are excellent choices because all contribute significant amounts of nitrogen to the soil in which they grow. Buckwheat, grains, and grasses are also good choices.

To plant a cover crop:

1. **Rake the bed, broadcast the seeds, and rake the bed again to slightly bury the seeds.**

2. **Water to keep the bed moist until the seedlings are well up.**

   Don't let the cover crop go to seed, or it can become a reseeding pest in the flowerbed.

3. **Mow off the tops and let the trimmings dry in place.**

4. **Till everything into the soil — roots and all — at least six weeks before you anticipate planting your flowers.**

Chapter 7

The Good Part: Buying and Planting Flowers

● ●

In This Chapter

▶ Ordering from nursery catalogs

▶ Shopping the local nurseries

▶ Finding and choosing the healthiest perennials

▶ Deciding when to plant

▶ The how-to's of planting

▶ Caring for the newly planted garden

● ●

After you develop a garden plan and finish building the flowerbed, the really fun part begins. Now you get to flip through catalogs and visit nurseries, choose from a dazzling array of flowers, and experience the amazing sense of accomplishment that comes from transforming a patch of bare dirt into a sensational flower garden.

Sending Away for Mail-Order Miracles

When my brothers and I were growing up, we eagerly anticipated the arrival of the Sears catalog each fall. We spent endless hours poring through this wish book, searching for that one perfect toy to make our lives complete.

As an adult, garden catalogs bring back much of that same thrill for me. Their mailings are cleverly timed to tempt gardeners at their most vulnerable — during the winter doldrums.

For the gardener socked in by inclement weather, looking at garden catalogs is the equivalent of grocery shopping on an empty stomach — it may be unwise but, boy, does everything look good. My garden is never more perfect than the virtual reality of my midwinter musings.

Finding catalogs

You may already receive several garden catalogs in the mail each winter and spring. Hundreds are available — from spartan typed lists with minimal descriptions and no illustrations to works of art filled with glamorous photographs that put glossy fashion magazines to shame. Some catalogs specialize in only one type of perennial; others present a vast array for every climate. The best ones are packed with information describing each plant, detailed cultural information, and design advice.

No nursery has the space to stock even a fraction of the thousands of perennials in cultivation. Mail-order sources are often the only way to locate the rare, the unusual, and the avant-garde of gardening.

Nearly every garden magazine advertises dozens of mail-order nurseries. Most mail-order nurseries require a small fee to send you their catalogs, but they usually refund the amount after you make your first purchase. Publishers and catalog companies share your name with competitors, so after you subscribe to a single garden magazine or send for the first catalog, more catalogs and magazine offers arrive as well.

Placing an order

You must exercise some prudence and caution when deciding which plants to order from a catalog. A few catalogs make exaggerated claims of performance, desirability, or hardiness. A little research often saves great disappointment later. Find out whether each perennial you have fallen in love with works in your climate. Losing your heart and your common sense to a pretty picture is all too easy.

My method for catalog ordering involves making a series of lists:

- ✔ The first list is a free-for-all of unfettered greed as I check off every remotely interesting and desirable plant in the catalog.

- ✔ After the first round, in which I usually circle or underline most of the catalog, I begin the process of weeding out. "No," I concede, "I probably won't get around to digging a bog this year, so those plants can go." "No, those eastern woodlanders probably won't adjust to my hot, arid region, and all those subtropical selections are probably pushing it a bit in my cold-climate garden." And so on.

- ✔ Then I subject the pared-down list to the calculator test. The shock of realization sets in when the total still exceeds the GNP of many small nations. The last list, the one that passes the reality check, is the one I actually send off.

Most mail-order nurseries have minimum shipping fees. Some have a flat fee per order; many have minimum order amounts. You can almost always save money on shipping costs when you get together with a group of friends and combine several orders. One clever bulb company, Dutch Gardens, encourages this practice by sending out several order blanks with each catalog.

Shipping considerations

Shipping plants has some inherent problems. The cost is high, and most nurseries try to keep the weight down by sending their plants either bare root or in small containers filled with lightweight, soil-less mix.

Bare-root plants are just that — plants whose roots have been unearthed and are completely, unabashedly exposed. Mailed with their roots packed in moistened moss or wood shavings and wrapped in newspaper or plastic, these plants are very fragile and perishable. They must not be allowed to dry out, but leaving them in their damp shipping material for very long encourages rotting.

The time of year that your plants are shipped and the shape they're in when you get them depend on what type of plants you order.

✔ Bare-root plants arrive in a dormant or semi-dormant state, usually in late winter or early spring.

✔ Bulbs and fleshy-rooted perennials are also shipped in summer and hardly seem to notice that they're out of the ground. Peonies, bearded iris, daylilies, hostas, and liatris don't object to this treatment in the least.

✔ In some cases, your perennials can arrive quite unhappy and indignant (no matter what time of year they're sent) and may require pampering for a full year to recover their former health and vigor.

Arrange for your plants to be shipped by the quickest option, especially during hot months when the poor plants can easily cook or dry out in transit. Ask that your order be sent at the proper planting time for your area and at a time when you can be at home to receive the package. Even plants that survive the initial journey don't last long if you leave them unattended on a hot porch.

When the plants arrive

On that great day when your plants finally arrive, unpack the box immediately in a cool, shaded location. Check off on the invoice each plant you unpack to make sure that your order is complete. Keep each label with its plant — green and brown lumps tend to look alike at this stage.

You can store plants shipped in pots for several days in a shady spot with plenty of indirect light. Be sure to water the pots whenever they dry out, but don't overwater them. If their bed isn't ready, you must find a temporary home for them. A vegetable garden is an ideal holding area for new perennials.

Many garden guides recommend *heeling in* bare-root plants. This process involves digging a trench, laying plants in it at a 30-degree angle, and covering the roots with soil. Heeling in works fine for shrubs but isn't a good practice for perennials. Flowers prefer you to plant them properly in their interim location and then transplant them later, after they establish strong new growth.

Raised bed with perennials of varying heights: 'Husker's red' beardtongue
(Penstemon digitalis 'Husker Red') with Delphinium

Fancy-leafed
caladium:
Caladium bicolor.

© DAVID CAVAGNARO

Purple coneflower:
Echinacea purpurea
and Globe thistle:
Echinops exaltatus.

© DAVID CAVAGNARO

Blue fescue: *Festuca glauca* with African lily: *Agapanthus.*

© DAVID CAVAGNARO

Blanket flower: *Gaillardia* 'Kobold.'

© DAVID CAVAGNARO

Shasta daisy: *Leucanthemum maximum* 'Shasta Snow.'

Blue flax: *Linum perenne.*

Lupine: *Lupinus* hybrid.

Peony: *Paeonia* 'Legion of Honor.'

© David Cavagnaro

© David Cavagnaro

Woodland phlox: *Phlox divaricata.*

Most mail-order nurseries send instructions with your order. File away these instructions away for future reference along with your receipt and invoice. Many companies guarantee their plants, and you need the paperwork to request a refund or replacement if the original plant fails. I always keep the catalogs, too, as a source of information and to cut up to make garden records. Notify the nursery right away of any problems. (Once, instead of the plant I ordered, I received a very healthy, carefully wrapped dandelion!)

Taking the Nursery Safari

Shopping for plants at a nursery is much like shopping for plants from a catalog, but with fewer restraints. In nurseries, the plants are harder to deny — they're right in front of you, most of them presumably perfectly compatible to your local climate and conditions. Self-control (and the limit on your credit card) can be sorely tested. Before you know it, you've filled one shopping cart to bulging and are seriously contemplating a second (and these are usually large carts!).

Whenever you have a choice between buying a plant by mail or from a local nursery, always go with the nursery. A plant purchased locally is almost always cheaper than one ordered by mail because you aren't paying those high shipping costs. The nursery plant is also usually healthier because it hasn't been subjected to the trauma of traveling — at least not recently. Most nurseries bring in some of their stock bare root in the winter and grow it in containers before offering it up for sale. This way, the nursery takes the risk, and you buy only those plants that survived and prospered. Also, at a nursery, you can actually see the plant you buy and can pick out the best of the batch.

Save catalogs for the perennials that you can't find locally — you'll discover plenty of those. A few perennials, such as daylilies, irises, hostas, and peonies, have hundreds of named varieties. A wider selection of these varieties is available by mail order, compared with only a few at each nursery.

Locating nurseries

Large nurseries and garden centers advertise in the Yellow Pages of the telephone book and in the garden section of the local newspaper. Small specialty growers can be harder to track down. Ask a gardener or call a regional plant society to find, for example, a daylily grower in your area.

Choose a nursery where the plants look healthy and the staff is knowledgeable and helpful. Many good nurseries offer gardening classes and employ a master gardener to answer your questions. They may also group plants by their cultural needs to help you decide what goes where. Shade plants are generally protected under some sort of structure.

When you purchase plants, ask about a guarantee and save your receipts. Many reputable nurseries don't warranty the plants, however, because what you do to the plant after you leave the store is out of their control.

Buying from discounters

With the burgeoning popularity of perennial gardening, many home improvement centers, supermarkets, and discount stores carry a wide variety of perennials. Sometimes, these discounters offer perennials as loss leaders, heavily discounted products sold as a marketing strategy to get you into the store.

Some real bargains are possible at non-nursery stores, but you're usually more or less on your own to determine which plants are the healthiest or what cultural conditions they require. Although some stores try to find informed help, others don't even seem to understand that plants need water to survive. Plants may be selected for a national market and can be entirely inappropriate for the regions where they end up. I cringe every time I see hapless subtropicals going home to a certain death and a disappointed gardener in hardly-subtropical Colorado.

On the other hand, I can't resist a bargain, and I suspect that you can't either. But do some homework first to make sure that the plants you buy have a ghost of a chance in your garden. Also, buy them as soon as they've been unloaded from the truck — hopefully before they've been mishandled or mistreated.

You can also find some great deals on nursery plants by watching for end-of-season clearance sales. Some of the plants are looking shop-worn by this time, but I figure that only the really strong-willed can survive several months on the sales bench. So these last plants, the rejected and overlooked, are usually worth the risk.

Getting the pick of the litter

When purchasing a perennial, look for one with a compact form and proportioned-to-the-pot size. Pass on any plants that are tall and leggy or flopping over to one side.

You want lean and mean, not overly lush. Check the foliage for any signs of disease. Don't buy plants that are wilted, yellowed, or mottled. Avoid plants that have orange, brown, or black spots or that have distorted or curled leaves. Flip a few leaves over to see whether tiny mites, aphids, or whiteflies reside there (see Chapter 12 for more on these critters). Look along the stems for scale insects. Don't be put off by a few holes made by chewing insects — these culprits are either long gone or large enough to remove easily.

Perennials come in many pot sizes. Occasionally, first-year seedlings are available in six-packs, the standard container for bedding annuals. These packages can be real money-savers when they contain varieties that mature quickly and bloom the first year from seed. Otherwise, you may have to wait a year or two to see the flowers. Perennials are more customarily sold in 2½-, 4-, and 6-inch containers. The larger plants are more expensive because they cost more to produce. Most nurseries start their perennials in small pots and move them up to larger ones as they outgrow each size. Some perennials have large, fleshy roots and are only available in 6-inch pots because they just don't fit in anything else.

Small plants are much easier to transplant — they require smaller holes, after all. But the trade-off is that the little ones need more care initially. They dry out faster and may need watering as often as twice a day until they're established and growing strongly.

Healthy roots mean healthy perennials

Healthy roots are just as important as the above-ground parts of the plant, but they're more difficult to assess. Judging roots involves a bit of detective work. A top-quality container plant has a vigorous root system that fills but doesn't outgrow its pot. Ideally, the volume of roots and soil is about 50/50.

You can get some idea of what condition a potted plant's roots are in by checking the surface of the soil. If you can see roots circling or trying to climb out, ask the clerk to remove the pot so that you can get a better look. Nurseries routinely turn their pots upside down to monitor root status, so this request won't seem odd to the clerk, although it may seem strange to you.

Excess roots can displace most of the soil in a container, making the plant root-bound, a condition that causes a couple of problems. First, without enough soil to retain water or fertilizer, the plants quickly start to suffer from drought stress. More importantly, the roots don't have anywhere to go, so they start to circle and grow into a tight ball.

Too few roots is just as bad a sign as too many. Reputable nurseries don't routinely sell perennials that are too recently transplanted, but occasionally a few slip through quality control. Roots should expand out at least to the edges of the container. If they don't, you're paying for a small plant and some very expensive potting soil. Carefully tip the pot over and look at the bottom. A few small roots should be visible at the drainage holes.

Reviewing the Planting Basics

In theory, you can plant container-grown perennials at any time of the year when the ground isn't frozen. But in reality, survival rates improve when you take your climate into consideration and schedule your planting accordingly. Newly transplanted perennials need a period of intensive care while they settle in and adjust to their new home. Strong sunshine, drying winds, and intense heat can stress any plant. These conditions are especially damaging to plants that have been recently disturbed and are busy repairing torn roots and coping with the inevitable trauma that transplanting causes.

Timing is critical

By planting at a time of year when you can count on the weather to be mild for a while, you give the garden a head start. In cold-winter regions, planting in early spring gives perennials a couple of months to get used to the climate before hot weather sets in. Only bulbs, bearded iris, peonies, and oriental poppies are safe to plant during the fall in the coldest winter regions. But in areas where winter temperatures don't fall below –20° F (–29° C), early fall is another excellent time to plant the flowerbed. Even though the days are shorter and cooler, root growth continues unimpeded after frost has blackened the top of the plant, not stopping until the ground freezes solidly.

Gardeners in mild coastal climates can plant their flower beds at any time of the year, whenever planting is convenient. In hot, humid, mild-winter regions, fall planting is preferable. Planting in fall enables perennials to grow strong root systems before they're subjected to the heat of summer.

Whatever time of year you decide to plant your flower bed, make sure that you can give it your full attention for several weeks afterward. A new garden needs vigilance — it's as needy as a new puppy. Check the flowers for wilting or other signs of distress at least twice a day until they start to put on new growth. Right after planting isn't a good time to leave for an extended vacation.

Hardening off

Hardening off is similar to the tanning routine that people had to put themselves through each spring before the invention of sunscreens. You probably remember lying out in the sun for a few minutes each day and gradually lengthening the exposure time until you could withstand several hours of sunshine without blistering. Your plants may need a similar routine to get accustomed to sunshine.

Plants that have been growing outside at the nursery can go right into the ground without a period of hardening off. But greenhouse-grown plants are lush and soft and have never known a single day of sunshine in their lifetimes. They must be introduced slowly to the harsh, real world.

Leave the plants in their containers and put them in a shaded area with some indirect light for a few days. A north-facing covered porch is ideal. Whenever a freeze is predicted, bring the plants inside overnight. If these are shade plants, you can leave them in this protected site for a few more days and then put them in the garden. For sunny-spot plants, give them a few days in the shaded area and then place the plants in a sunny location for an hour one day. Give them a couple of hours of sun the next day, and so on, increasing their exposure each day. At the end of a week, the plants are thoroughly accustomed to sunlight and wind and are ready to go into their new home.

If you don't have time for all this hardening-off nonsense, simply buy plants that the nursery has had growing outside for at least a while (ask if you have any doubts about which ones have been outside or for how long).

Picking the perfect day to plant

To get your plants off to a vigorous start, you need to choose your planting day carefully. In some parts of the country, the perfect day is such a rarity that calling in sick to take advantage of it is justifiable. In other regions, every day is a good day.

You're looking for a cool, overcast day, preferably the first of many with no record-breaking heat predicted for the near future. An imminent threat of a rainstorm is better yet, if you can get your bed finished before the storm strikes. If cooperative weather is not in the forecast, plant early in the morning or in the evening.

Digging In — It's Showtime!

After you choose a spot for your garden, prepare your soil, purchase your plants, and harden them off (if necessary), the big day finally arrives. Put on some old clothes, get out a pair of gardening gloves and a shovel (and maybe a bottle of champagne), and prepare to get dirty!

If your flower bed is wider than you can easily reach across, lay some old boards or some stepping stones throughout the area. Standing on these additions keeps you off the fluffy soil.

Distribute container plants, following your plan — if you've made one. Mark spots for bulbs and bare-root perennials with empty pots or stakes. Make certain that you've allowed adequate spacing for each plant to spread to its mature size; the nursery tag often has this information. Take note of where you need to add annuals for temporary fill until the perennials actually use their allotted space.

Planting potted perennials

Planting a potted perennial is easy with a little practice. Make a copy of these instructions to take into the garden with you (or write them on the back of your hand). Keep the instructions with you until you have the knack. Plant the largest pots first; the smaller ones are easier to tuck in afterwards. Finish planting each perennial before going on to the next.

1. **Dig a hole for the plant using a shovel or a spade.**

   Make the hole at least double the diameter of the pot. (See Figure 7-1.)

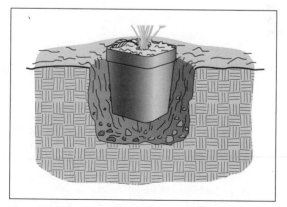

Figure 7-1: Dig a hole large enough to fit in the plant's roots without crowding.

2. Remove the plant from the pot.

This step isn't always as simple as it sounds. When things are going well, you cradle the top of the plant between the fingers of one hand, tip the pot upside down, and slip the plant out to rest snugly against the palm of the opposite hand. (See Figure 7-2.)

Figure 7-2: Getting a plant out of its pot.

However, often the plant refuses to budge. If this happens, try rapping the bottom of the pot smartly with your unoccupied hand. If that attempt fails, lay the plastic pot on its side on the ground and gently step on and compress the pot just a little. Next, give the pot a quarter turn and step on it again. Whatever you do, don't try to pull the plant out by its top. The top usually breaks off in your hand — instead of liberating the plant, you kill it.

Small pots can usually be coaxed into releasing their contents by pinching and poking through the bottom of the pot. You can also tear off a small pot. When these other options fail, cut the pot off with heavy-duty shears — which is not as easy as it sounds and should always be the last resort.

3. Place the plant gently into the hole.

You want the *crown* of the plant — where the top of
the plant meets the roots — at ground level, as shown
in Figure 7-3, so you need to adjust the soil level until
the *root ball* sits at about the right height. Don't bury
the crown or lower leaves. Break off any layer of moss
or crud on the surface of the soil surrounding the
plant. (You can drop whatever you break off into the
hole for extra soil nutrients.)

Check for and remove weeds. Also look for slug eggs
— masses of tiny clear balls — and dispose of them.
(See Chapter 12 for more on slug solutions.) Tease a
few roots away from the root ball. Try to straighten
out any large, fibrous roots. If the hole isn't large
enough for a relaxed fit for the roots, remove the
plant, enlarge the hole, and try again.

Figure 7-3: Plant the perennial at the same depth as in its container.

4. Fill the hole back up with dirt.

Fan out the plant's roots in the hole. Hold the plant
with the crown at the proper height with one hand and
start refilling the hole with the other hand. Add a
handful of dirt at a time, breaking up large chunks as

you go. You don't want to leave huge holes underground because the roots need to be in direct contact
with the soil.

Pat the soil around the plant carefully. No stamping of
feet is allowed, especially on clay soils. Remember
that you want 25 percent of the soil to be air pockets
when you're finished (see Chapter 6 for details). Check
to make sure that all the roots are underground and all
the leaves are above the surface.

5. **Water the plant.**

   With a watering can or a hose turned on very low, sat-
   urate the newly planted area with water. Some of the
   soil always collapses inward at this point, so add more
   as necessary. If the whole plant sinks, carefully pull it
   back up again and push some more soil underneath
   the root ball.

6. **Label the plant.**

   Use the plastic nursery label or make a homemade
   label. Push the label about two-thirds of the way into
   the soil near the crown of each plant, so that you can
   find it when necessary but it isn't particularly visible
   otherwise.

7. **Feed the plant.**

   Pour a weak solution of manure tea or liquid fertilizer
   mixed at one-fourth the usual strength recommended
   on the label. Use just enough of the solution to reach
   the soil at the base of the plant. This first feeding
   helps improve the perennial's chances of survival.

8. **Move on to the next plant, repeating Steps 1 through
   7.**

9. **Spread the mulch last, after you have watered,
   labeled, and fed all the perennials.**

   If you plan to use a mulch (as described in Chapter
   11), apply it immediately after planting so that weeds
   don't get a running start in the bare soil.

10. **Get yourself a piece of cheesecake (or open up that
    bottle of champagne).**

    You've earned a reward!

Breaking up root balls

Occasionally, you bring home a root-bound plant despite your best efforts to avoid them. Maybe it's the only one of that particular plant in the whole city or it may be an end-of-season bargain. If you plant the root ball intact, you may find it in the same shape and size when you dig up the carcass two years later. You can succeed with root-bound plants, but you need to treat them very roughly before you plant them.

Break apart the root ball as much as you can, untangling the largest roots as you go. Sometimes the only way to do so is to butterfly the root ball. Lay it on the ground and cut the root ball in two, approximately two-thirds of the way toward the crown. Spread the two sides apart and plant with the roots in this position.

Planting "exceptional" perennials

A few varieties of perennials require special planting techniques. They may have special kinds of roots or prefer to be planted with their crowns deeper than ground level. Here are some specifics on a few common perennials that need a little special treatment:

✔ **Bearded iris:** Iris plants have a swollen, fleshy root called a *rhizome*. Green leaves, called a *fan,* protrude from the bottom. To plant an iris, dig a large shallow hole and build up a center cone of soil. Place the rhizome against the cone with the fan facing outward and the roots spread out and downward. If you're planting several rhizomes of the same iris, place the fans in a circle around the soil cone.

Press soil over the roots and the rhizomes to keep the fans from falling down. Barely cover the rhizome with soil in cold climates. Leave the rhizomes partially exposed in warm, wet regions to improve the drainage.

✔ **Peonies:** Herbaceous peonies are an exception to the general rule of planting the crown of a perennial at soil level. Peonies prefer to be planted with their *eyes,* the buds emerging from the crown, 1 to 2 inches (2.5 to 3 cm) below the surface of the soil. If you plant them any deeper, peonies often fail to bloom.

✔ **Oriental poppies:** Oriental poppies like to be planted deeply with their crown buried 3 inches (8 cm) deep (measured from the top of the crown to the surface of the soil).

Planting bare-root perennials

The first time you unwrap a package of bare-root perennials, you're probably in for a bit of a shock. Often, the whole shipment appears to be dead. Both the roots and the tops are brown when the plants are in a dormant state, and sometimes you can hardly tell what end goes up. You may find swollen buds or remnants of dead leaves at the crown of the plant, or fleshy roots may look more alive than the top. If you really can't tell the top from the bottom, call the nursery that you ordered from for advice.

To plant bare-root perennials, follow these steps:

1. **Carefully unwrap and remove the packing material.**

2. **Soak the roots in a bucket of water for a few hours or overnight.**

   Don't cover the whole plant, just the roots.

3. **Dig a roomy hole.**

   Build a cone of soil in the center of the hole.

4. **Spread the roots over the cone.**

5. **Refill the hole.**

   Hold the crown of the plant at the soil level and form the soil around the roots with your fingers.

6. **Water the plant evenly and fill any sinkholes with additional garden soil.**

Protecting new transplants

Sometimes, the weather forecaster turns out to be wrong, and the promised cloud cover burns off. Your new garden is now faced with full sun and rapidly rising temperatures, and you must create temporary shelter quickly.

What to do with all those pots

After you finish planting your garden, you may wonder what to do with all those plastic pots. Most nurseries happily take back their pots and trays for reuse. They usually don't want the empty four-packs or six-packs, but you can use those for starting seeds. Or you can find gardening friends or neighbors who grow most of their own flowers or vegetables from seed. They're usually delighted to recycle your discards.

Placing evergreen boughs in a tent around the plant, stems poked into the ground and tips facing inward, does an effective job of protecting individual plants. You can overlap boughs to cover a whole flower bed if the plants aren't tall enough to be smashed down by the boughs. My favorite material is one of the new lightweight, spun-bonded landscape fabrics. Simply spread this fabric over the flower bed and anchor down the corners with stones or other heavy objects. These materials are porous, so you can leave them in place for as long as you need — water and air pass through readily.

No matter how careful you are, you may very well lose a few of your newly planted perennials. The reason why is usually a mystery. You may have two identical plants placed only inches apart — one lives, the other dies. Some plants just don't seem to have a strong will to live.

What kills most newly planted perennials is transplant shock. Its symptoms are leafs and flowers that drop and wilt — even when the soil is damp.

Don't water a plant exhibiting signs of transplant shock without first checking the root ball to see whether it is dry. Overwatering usually hastens the demise of a plant in this situation. Shelter the plant for a few days, cross your fingers, and hope for the best. Burning candles at the altar or repeating a mantra may not hurt, either. Most plants recover — even plants that appear dead can come back the following spring from live roots. Don't be too hasty to give a perennial the 10-count.

Chapter 8

Grab Your Watering Can

. . . .

In This Chapter

▶ Choosing a watering device

▶ Deciding when to water

▶ Avoiding problems from over- and underwatering

▶ Getting water to the roots

▶ Conserving water

. . . .

*F*iguring out how to water effectively and efficiently is the trickiest part of the whole gardening maintenance routine. It's the old "Goldilocks and the Three Bears" conundrum. Overwatering drowns your perennials; underwatering causes them to dry up and get crispy. Determining how much water is "just right" is the challenge.

Determining a Plant's Water Needs

How much water each perennial requires to stay fit and healthy depends on a number of factors:

✔ **Climate:** In climates where rainfall is regular and reliable, watering isn't a pressing need, except during occasional prolonged dry spells or drought. (Every climate undergoes a dry spell periodically. I was quite surprised to experience two hosepipe bans, during which watering the garden was forbidden, due to drought during the four years I lived in generally drizzly England.)

In arid regions, irrigation is often an all-consuming activity. Watering becomes the garden's artificial life-support system. Ironically, the same perennial that insists on frequent irrigation to survive in a hot, dry environment may rot in a wet climate.

✔ **Weather:** Climate is determined by average prevailing weather conditions; weather is what's happening outside as you read this. Out-of-the-ordinary weather can wreak havoc on your plants. Windstorms and high temperatures can dry out a garden very quickly. My carefully tended fern garden in Southern California was burned to the ground, in a manner of speaking, in one afternoon of hot desert winds.

✔ **Soil types:** Different soil types also affect how often the garden needs water. Sand holds moisture about as efficiently as a sieve. Water penetrates sandy soil readily and deeply but tends to filter right on through. Heavy clay is the exact opposite. Its dense soil particles crust over and deflect water drops. Water applied slowly and in stages soaks in; water applied quickly just runs off. But after clay is saturated, it holds water very well — sometimes so well that the plants rot.

Add organic matter to cure both sandy and clayey conditions. Sandy soil that has been amended retains water better; organic matter breaks up clay and improves its drainage. (See Chapter 6 for more information on soil types and amending soils with organic matter.)

✔ **Location, location, location:** In general, shaded gardens need less water than gardens in the full blast of the midday sun. However, in places where trees are responsible for casting the shadow, their roots may greedily grab water, outcompeting the flowers. In this situation, sometimes no amount of water is ever enough to satisfy both the trees and the flowers.

✔ **Genetic disposition:** Some plants are splendidly adaptable, enduring swamp or desert with equal aplomb. But most plants prefer some approximation of their natural habitat. Plants from wet places generally need more water than plants from dry places. This rule may seem quite obvious, but many gardening disasters result from a failure to follow it. (See the sidebar, "Grouping plants according to their needs.")

Getting Water to the Garden

Watering cans are a good short-term measure for new transplants, and standing in the garden with your thumb over the end of a hose may be relaxing and give you a sense of accomplishment. But neither method is satisfactory for providing the thorough soaking an established garden needs.

The three primary methods for irrigating flowerbeds are the following:

✔ **The portable system:** You probably already know the old hose-and-sprinkler routine all too well. The advantage is the low cost — one hose and one sprinkler at the bare minimum. The drawbacks, however, are legion — rolling out the hose and moving the sprinkler from place to place is always a chore, and water coverage is generally poor. Tall plants block the water spray either to their own roots or to their bedmates behind (see Figure 8-1).

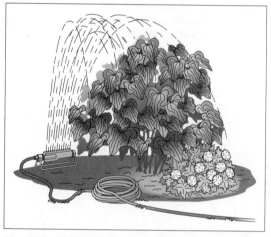

Figure 8-1: Taller growth sometimes blocks spray from a sprinkler, causing dry spots in the back of the flowerbed.

Sprinklers work best when every flower is the same height. Most sprinklers spray in uneven patterns, so don't place them in the same spot each time.

Sprinklers wet the foliage, which may spread diseases in the flower bed, making them a bad choice in hot, humid climates. But in hot, dry climates, wetting the foliage rinses dust off the leaves and helps prevent spider mite infestations.

✔ **Drip irrigation:** Two main types of drip irrigation are available: leaky hoses and individual emitters. Leaky hoses are either porous tubes manufactured from old tires or flat tapes with slits cut at intervals. You can lay either kind directly on top of the soil under the mulch (as shown in Figure 8-2), or bury them a few inches deep. I prefer the first method so that I can easily get to the hose to repair the inevitable geysers. Leaky-hose products I've used have been uneven in water distribution, especially on hillsides, but they're still my favorite method for irrigating flower beds.

In another type of drip irrigation system, you wind rigid plastic tubing through the flower bed. You place the individual emitters that are attached to the line directly on the root ball of each perennial. This system is highly efficient at delivering water. Keep in mind, though, that every new plant needs its own emitter.

Figure 8-2: Snake leaky hoses back and forth between the plants in the flowerbed.

✔ **The automated system:** Automatic systems can be real time-savers and can give you freedom to safely take a vacation in the middle of summer (with only an overseer — possibly the kid next door — to ensure that the system is actually working while you're away). You can even purchase built-in timers or moisture sensors so that the system comes on when needed, rather than on a fixed schedule. Both sprinklers and drip irrigation can be fully automated.

Grouping plants according to their needs

In Colorado, landscapers love the look of pines and aspen trees growing together. The problem is that aspens like constant moisture and pines need to be relatively dry. Eventually, one or the other always dies because their cultural needs are just too incompatible. A neighborhood near me replaces a dozen expensive 10-foot pines every single year because the trees die from too much water.

The one most important factor in creating a successful garden is grouping plants that have the same cultural needs so that you can tend to them as a group, rather than individually. Build separate flower beds for flowers with dissimilar needs, and each bed can have its own personalized schedule for watering and other maintenance tasks.

Deciding When to Water

Most perennials require water only after the top few inches of soil dry out, but before the plant starts to show symptoms of drought stress. Perennials from arid habitats benefit when the dry interval between waterings is longer. Plants from wet places prefer to never completely dry out.

Problems occur when the soil is either too wet or too dry for too long. But, just to complicate matters, overwatered and underwatered perennials exhibit nearly identical symptoms. Both conditions cause plants to wilt and droop miserably, to develop yellowed leaves with brown edges, and to experience stunted growth. Flowers and leaves start to drop off, and eventually the pitiful thing just dies. You can't tell by looking whether too much or too little water is the culprit. Your first inclination may be to just grab a hose or watering can. But you must actually feel the soil to be certain whether the soil is too wet or too dry.

Don't simply feel the surface of the soil to check for over- or underwatering. The top few inches can be deceptively different from the soil underneath. When your perennials first start to show signs of stress, dig a small hole several inches deep and feel the soil. If the soil's wet, you know that you need to cut back on water. If the soil is dry, water more frequently.

Clay is more difficult to judge than sand. The tiny clay particles can grab hold of moisture so tightly that the soil can feel cool and somewhat moist, and yet the plants can't get the water. Amending clay soil with plenty of organic matter alleviates this problem (see Chapter 6 for more on amending soils).

You can buy an electronic moisture monitor to help you decide when to water. Or you can use a long screwdriver as a low-tech soil probe. If you can easily push the screwdriver deeply into the soil, your garden probably has enough moisture.

Accounting for seasonal variations

After one season of careful monitoring, you start to get a sense of how often your garden wants water. At this point, you can safely begin to use an automatic timer for the sake of convenience. But don't set the timer in the spring and leave it unchanged for the whole growing season. A plant's water demands change with the seasons.

Adequate and even moisture is essential for most perennials during their spring growth spurt. But many regions have special watering needs:

- ✔ Mediterranean flowers and others from coastal regions often require a summer dormancy period and must be kept fairly dry during their nap. During the summer, give them only an infrequent deep soaking when the soil is completely dry.

- ✔ In regions with cold winters, always start lengthening the intervals between waterings in late summer to toughen your plants for winter (a process that gardeners call *hardening off*). You don't want your perennials to face the first frost with lush, easily damaged new growth.

- ✔ Where winters are cold and dry, the garden benefits from a drink once a month, whenever it hasn't rained or snowed for a few weeks. Water your garden on a day when temperatures are above freezing and the surface of the soil is thawed so that the water doesn't simply run off.

Considering the time of day

An old adage warns never to water during the middle of a sunny day, lest the water droplets burn the foliage like a magnifying glass. I have doubts about this warning (although salt residue left from rapid evaporation may burn the leaves). The real reason you shouldn't water in the hottest part of the day is efficiency. Much of the water from a midday watering evaporates before it has a chance to soak in. The same goes for watering when a wind is blowing. Watering in the evening or early morning is preferable wherever you live, but keep in mind the following tips:

- ✔ Water whenever the soil is dry and plants are wilting or showing signs of imminent death. Most perennials wilt on a hot day, regardless of whether or not they need water. Water only when the soil is dry and the plants don't recover from their "faint" overnight.

- ✔ You're usually better off watering in the morning than in the evening. Mornings aren't as windy as evenings, so less water gets blown away. Also, the moisture from a morning watering recharges your plants for the day.

- ✔ In tropical regions, wet foliage may help spread some diseases. If you live in a steamy, damp climate, it's especially important to water early in the morning so that leaves dry off quickly as the day heats up.

- ✔ If you live in a dry region, watering in the evening gives plants ample time to absorb the water overnight.

Taking care of new transplants

Newly transplanted perennials are especially vulnerable in the first few weeks. Extra pampering gets them off to a good, strong start. Little root balls can dry out very quickly. During really hot spells, you may need to water more than once a day. Water new transplants every time their roots dry out, whether the surrounding soil is still damp or not. The only way you can tell whether the root ball is dry is to push your fingers into the soil at the base of each plant and feel for yourself.

A process called *wicking* can cause a newly planted root ball to remain absolutely dry, even while standing in a puddle of mud. Wicking can occur whenever two different types of soil meet. The soil in the prepared flower bed is almost always heavier and denser than the potting mix surrounding the root ball. Moisture is pulled out of the light soil, leaving the new plant high and dry. After a few weeks, the roots travel out into the new soil, and the problem is solved. But in the meantime, you must make certain that the root ball is actually getting wet.

Here's a good, low-tech, temporary, and free method you can use to water new transplants. This process creates an all-day, automatic drip system.

1. **Rinse out a 1-gallon (2-liter) plastic bottle or jug.**

2. **Using a needle, poke a small hole in the bottom near a corner.**

   You want a very slow drip, so that it takes several days for all the water to drain out of the container.

3. **Fill the container with water.**

4. **Set the container next to a newly transplanted perennial.**

5. **Refill the container as needed.**

   Leave the container in place until the plant puts on several inches of new growth.

Watering cans are another easy way to take care of your transplants' watering needs. Choose a can with a soft spray attachment. A hard splash can wash away soil and expose the tender roots.

Knowing How Much to Water

Perennials generally spread most of their roots in the top 12 inches (30 cm) of the soil, although roots may grow deeper in sandy, fast-draining soils and more shallowly in clay. Watering a few inches deeper than this root zone encourages roots to dive deeper, where they're protected from fluctuating surface temperatures. Roots grow best at constant, cool temperatures, and shallow-rooted perennials dry out too quickly and must be watered more frequently.

You can't tell how deeply the water is penetrating by looking at the surface of the soil. The only way to tell whether the water is soaking down deeper than the roots is to dig a few test holes and check. The best method for determining how long to water your garden is to follow these steps:

1. **Wait until your soil is fairly dry at least 6 inches (15 cm) deep.**

2. **Set up whatever system you plan to use (whether sprinkler or soaker hose) and water the flower bed for a set period of time — say 30 minutes.**

3. **Some time the next day, dig a hole to check how deep the soil is wet.**

   Use a narrow-bladed trowel to dig a small hole only 2 to 3 inches (5 to 7 cm) wide. Make the hole 1 foot (30 cm) away from the base of a plant. Don't worry if you cut into the roots — they grow back.

4. **If 30 minutes wasn't long enough to wet the soil 10 to 12 inches (26 to 30 cm) deep, let the soil dry out for a few days and water again — longer this time, say 45 minutes — and dig another hole.**

5. **Repeat this exercise until you discover just how long you need to run the water to get the soil wet to a depth of 1 foot (30 cm).**

   Different irrigation systems deliver water at varying rates, so retest whenever you change to a new sprinkler, hose, or system.

Watering too shallowly is wasteful because most of the water evaporates quickly, before the plants get a chance to quench their thirst. Watering too deeply is also wasteful because roots can only go so far down.

Cutting Down on Water Waste

Water shortages are a reality in any climate and region, and bans on watering are not uncommon. The following list outlines a few things that you can do when water is scarce or limited, when you want to reduce your water bill, or when you just want to conserve the precious resource of fresh water.

✔ **Turn off the water.** This piece of advice may seem obvious, but it's easy to leave a sprinkler running and then get busy and forget to turn it off. Set an egg timer to remind you or buy a faucet timer that automatically shuts off the water.

✔ **Choose a drip-irrigation method.** Sprinklers waste a great deal of water, throwing much of it into the air where it either evaporates or is blown away.

✔ **Collect rainwater.** A barrel like the one in Figure 8-3 collects rainwater from the gutters and holds it until you need it.

Figure 8-3: To catch rainwater, place a barrel at the end of a rainspout.

✔ **Divert rainwater.** Divert the rainwater from downspouts to flower beds by using French drains and pits filled with gravel. A *French drain* is simply an underground plastic pipe, sometimes with holes along the sides, that directs the water flow from the drainspout to the garden.

✔ **Mulch the garden.** Mulch helps hold water in the soil (see Chapter 11 for more details).

✔ **Irrigate deeply.** If you water too shallowly, most of the moisture evaporates before the plants can get it (see "Knowing How Much to Water," earlier in this chapter).

✔ **Measure rainfall.** Use a rain gauge to keep track of rainfall. If you have a fixed watering schedule, skip a watering whenever you record ½ inch (1 cm) or more of rain.

✔ **Plant a water-conserving garden.** Choose flowers that can get by on the average rainfall in your area. Then you can skip the chore of watering entirely, except while getting the perennials adjusted to their new flower bed and during occasional dry periods. (See Chapter 2 for details on this type of gardening, called *xeriscaping*.)

Chapter 9

Fertilizer: Food for Your Flowers

*J*ust like people, plants need vitamins and minerals in the right amounts to maintain good health. Unfortunately, choosing the right fertilizer is much like shopping for vitamins. The store shelves are lined with a dazzling array of products, and you don't know which one to choose.

You don't need a degree in chemistry to pick the right fertilizer for your perennials. You just need to know a few basics to make sense of all the muddle surrounding fertilizers. This chapter can help you make an intelligent purchase.

Vitamins for Your Garden

Research has identified 17 essential elements that plants must have for proper growth. Plants automatically get adequate supplies of carbon, hydrogen, and oxygen from water and air, so you don't have to worry about those three. Sunlight provides free fuel for *photosynthesis* — the process plants use to feed themselves. Everything else comes from the soil. When the soil is deficient in any of the remaining elements, you must replenish them or your flowers suffer.

Fertilizing your garden is the way you remedy the problem of malnourished soil. A *fertilizer* is any natural or manufactured material that you add to the soil in order to supply plant nutrients.

All perennials use up relatively large amounts of three primary nutrients: nitrogen, phosphorus, and potassium. In fact, many fertilizers contain only these three elements. Products containing all three are called complete, even if they are missing any or all of the remaining 11 elements.

Perennials need secondary nutrients (calcium, magnesium, and sulfur) in smaller amounts, and micronutrients (iron, manganese, copper, zinc, boron, molybdenum, chlorine, and cobalt) in still smaller quantities. Like the primary nutrients, these elements are essential for robust plant growth, but they are less likely than the primary nutrients to be deficient in your soil. Some commercial formulas add a selection of these other elements for extra insurance. The label often says "with iron" or "with micronutrients" to indicate their presence in the mixture.

You don't have to have a degree in chemistry to garden, but you do need to know that all plant nutrients are forms of salt. Just as too much salt in your diet isn't good for you, too much fertilizer is harmful to your plants. The salt concentration in the soil pulls water from the plant's roots, mimicking the effects of too little water. Consequently, the plants appear scorched even when the surrounding soil is wet.

Coping with nutrient shortages

A shortage of any nutrient eventually leads to problems. Plants exhibit a variety of symptoms, but the most common symptoms are slowed and stunted growth and pale, yellowish, or otherwise discolored foliage.

Fortunately, if you amended your soil with plenty of organic matter (following the guidelines in Chapter 6), it probably contains all the micronutrients your flowers will ever need. But the primary nutrient nitrogen is the one your garden depletes most quickly. Plants and microorganisms consume relatively large quantities of nitrogen, and it washes out of the soil more quickly than other nutrients. You generally need to add nitrogen to your perennial garden every year.

Shortages of elements vary by region. Also, different elements may be inadequate or unavailable to your perennials where the pH is either high or low (see Chapter 6 for more on pH). Here's where a soil test proves its worth. It tells you exactly which elements your soil already carries in sufficient amounts and which are lacking. Use a home test kit (available at most garden centers) or a professional soil testing lab (call the nearest agricultural university for a list of labs). Directions that come with the soil test results tell you precisely what fertilizers to add and in what amount, freeing you completely from guesswork. My soil, for example, is high in potassium, so I don't add more. Too much fertilizer throws things out of whack just as badly as too little. The goal is to create a balance.

Reading the label

In order to decide which fertilizer to buy, you must first figure out how to decipher those intimidating labels. Some standardization of information exists, but every company chooses to present the information in its own way. Somewhere on every package are the manufacturer's name, address, the product's name, the guaranteed analysis of the contents, a list of ingredients, and the weight. Most packages also include directions and suggestions for using the product — such as how much to apply, when, and how. To get an idea of what a fertilizer label looks like, see Figure 9-1.

 The three prominently displayed numbers separated by dashes and the section labeled guaranteed analysis below them tell you the percentages of nitrogen, phosphorus, and potassium the package contains by weight and volume. Nitrogen is always the first number, phosphorus the second, and potassium the third. (If any of these three elements is not in the formula, its spot contains a 0.) So, for example, a 100-pound bag of fertilizer marked 10-10-10 has 10 pounds (or 10 percent) of actual nitrogen.

 A 10-10-10 fertilizer is called complete because it contains all three primary nutrients in sufficient quantities to be of value as nutrients. The numbers 10-10-10 refer to the guaranteed analysis, or grade.

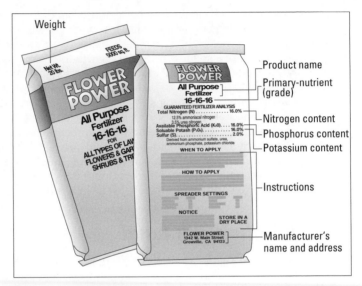

Figure 9-1: A fertilizer label.

If you're the thrifty type, you're probably wondering why you would buy a 100-pound bag of fertilizer if it only contains 30 pounds of nutrients. Good question. The answer can get complicated, but from a gardener's point of view, convenience is a major factor. More concentrated fertilizers are more difficult to apply because a little too much here or there can do more harm than good. Also, the other 70 pounds sometimes include other nutrients that benefit soils and plants.

Fertilizers are sometimes marketed especially for certain flowers. For example, you can find rose or rhododendron food. Generally, these specialty products are more expensive than all-purpose fertilizers — and, honestly, the rose doesn't know the difference. Compare products with and without the extras, and the cost of buying micronutrients separately. Then buy whatever is cheapest and still meets your needs.

In some regions, fertilizers are marketed to meet local conditions. These products can be helpful if your garden suffers from the targeted defects. In Colorado, for example, many brands add iron because iron tends to be deficient in this area's soils.

Forms of Fertilizer

Commercial fertilizer products are available in many diverse forms. You may need to try out several different kinds until you find the one you like to use.

✔ **Granular:** You can purchase both *synthetics* (man-made) and *organics* (natural materials) in granular form. Granular is usually the least expensive type of fertilizer. It's also moderately fast-acting and the most widely available form of fertilizer.

✔ **Pellets:** The pelleted forms of fertilizer look like colored BBs. Many brands are coated with resin or polymer so that they dissolve gradually and are available to the plants for a longer period of time. Most pellet fertilizers need to be applied only once a season. Because they release their nutrients slowly, less fertilizer is wasted and washed away before your perennials can grab what they need. These products are more costly than granular forms.

✔ **Solid tablets and spikes:** Tablets and spikes are made of compressed fertilizer. Pushed into the soil at intervals, the nutrients they contain tend to stay in concentrations high enough to burn and kill plant roots. Your goal is to spread the fertilizer as evenly as possible throughout the garden — which is impossible with these products.

✔ **Liquids and soluble powders:** Synthetic fertilizers and organics such as manure teas, seaweed extracts, and fish emulsions are available premixed and ready to apply. They also come in liquid or soluble powdered concentrations that you mix with water. All can be sprayed directly onto the foliage, where they are quickly absorbed. Liquid fertilizers are the fastest treatment for a nutrient deficiency, but they're short-acting and may need to be applied several times during the growing season. You can also spray them onto the ground. These fertilizers are fairly expensive.

✔ **Chelated minerals:** The word *chelated* on a fertilizer label means that this mineral has been specially processed so that plants can absorb it more efficiently. Chelated products are expensive, but they're worth the extra cost because they last longer.

✔ **Bulk organics:** Organic fertilizers come from diverse sources such as animal manure, sewage sludge, plant and animal residues, and mined minerals. Most contain nutrients in much lower concentrations than the synthetics, but they have some real benefits. Organics improve soil texture, hold water in the soil, and support communities of earthworms and microorganisms.

You can buy most organics either bagged or in bulk. Generally, you apply organic fertilizer as a top-dressing — 1 to 2 inches (3 to 5 cm) spread, once in the spring and once in the fall, directly over the mulch or soil, where the materials can filter down into the soil.

✔ **Designer fertilizers:** Chunks of manure shaped into decorative forms are all the rage as gifts for the gardener who has everything. These sculptures are cute but expensive methods of applying fertilizer. The preceding information on "bulk organics" applies to these products, as well.

✔ **Weed-and-feed products:** Be careful not to accidentally use weed-and-feed products on your perennial garden. These products are formulated for lawn care and kill most garden flowers just as they kill weeds. I know — once, under the influence of the flu, I picked up a bag of weed-and-feed by mistake and scattered it all over my flower beds. Plants started dying left and right before I realized what I'd done. If you ever make this mistake, the remedy is flooding the garden with large quantities of water to rinse out the herbicide.

When to Fertilize

Some gardeners fertilize every couple of weeks throughout the growing season, no matter what. Such compulsive behavior usually isn't necessary and can actually be harmful. Flowers getting excessive nitrogen, for example, may stop blooming altogether and just put on new foliage instead. Overdoing organic fertilizer is more difficult because it isn't as concentrated as synthetics.

If your soil test indicates a shortage, add the missing nutrient at least once a year, in spring, using either a synthetic or an organic fertilizer. Watch your flowers for clues that all is not well. If they don't seem to be actively growing or if they become pale or discolored, give them a shot of liquid fertilizer, and they should perk up.

A sample fertilizing routine

When, how, and how much you fertilize depends on your particular flower bed, but the general procedure is about the same for all gardeners. My fertilizer routine is typical.

My soil was originally low in nitrogen and phosphorus. When I amended each bed (as described in Chapter 6), I added phosphorus. This mineral is quite stable in the soil, so I won't need to add it in large amounts again soon. Nitrogen is the mineral my garden uses up quickly. I buy a high-nitrogen product in a slow-release pelleted form and spread it throughout my flower beds once a year in the spring. To provide micronutrients, I also top-dress with manure or compost once in the spring and once in the fall.

My soil's pH is extremely high, so occasionally a few flowers start to look sickly yellow. When this occurs, I spray a soil acidifier on the foliage for a quick fix. (I really should eliminate the problem by digging out the finicky flowers, but I don't have the heart!) I test my soil every couple of years just to make sure that everything's going well.

If you don't want to mess around with a soil test, simply apply a complete, balanced product formulated for general garden use (or for flower beds) once a year, in early spring. To make sure that your garden has enough micronutrients, also top-dress it twice a year with compost or well-aged manure (at least one year old or not too strong-smelling — if it burns your eyes, it will burn your plants!).

How to Fertilize

Always read the entire label and follow the directions carefully. Treat all fertilizers with care. Many can irritate your lungs if you breathe in the dust or can burn your skin or eyes upon contact. Wear gloves, eye protection, and a dust mask when handling any fertilizer. Store all fertilizers out of reach of children and pets — just as you do all other household chemical products.

Fertilizers that contain iron sulfate stain concrete walks and driveways, so sweep up any spilled granules or pellets. Dilute spilled liquids with water.

All fertilizers are salts and can burn plants if used improperly. The best time to apply most fertilizers is on an overcast, cool day or in the morning or late afternoon. Some fertilizers — especially ones that are water soluble or that contain a high percentage of nutrients — are more likely to burn plants on hot days than on cool days. Don't apply more fertilizer than the manufacturer recommends.

Using liquid and soluble powders

The goal when using liquid fertilizers is to wet the entire plant and the soil beneath. These products are absorbed quickly through the leaves and then more gradually through the roots.

To apply to small areas, mix the appropriate amount in a watering can. Hose-end sprayers (see Figure 9-2) are real time-savers when fertilizing large gardens. Some packages include a sprayer with the fertilizer. You can purchase refills later as you need them.

Figure 9-2: Apply liquid fertilizer to individual flowers with a watering can or spray the whole flower using a hose-end sprayer.

Applying granules and pellets

Because the nutrients from fertilizer granules and pellets are absorbed by the roots, they are more effective when you scratch them into the soil around the base of the plant. You can mix the fertilizer into the soil before planting your perennials or, after your flower bed is growing, follow these steps:

✔ For small gardens, spread the granules or pellets around the base of each plant and then scratch them into the top 1 to 2 inches (2 to 5 cm) of the soil, using a three-prong cultivator tool or a trowel.

✔ For large gardens, you can toss the fertilizer out of a bucket by hand (wearing gloves). But using a hand-held crank-type spreader (called a broadcaster), as shown in Figure 9-3, is easier, faster, and gives a more even application. You can buy a hand-held spreader at any garden center or hardware store.

Figure 9-3: Broadcasting fertilizer pellets with a mechanical spreader.

Spread the fertilizer right on top of the soil or mulch. Then water well to wash off any pellets that landed on leaves and so that the roots of the plants can absorb the fertilizer.

Chapter 10

Keeping Your Flowers in Tip-Top Shape

Some maintenance tasks require devotion to a regular routine during the blooming season to keep your flowers looking good. Other chores — such as getting the flower bed ready for winter — are seasonal. If you've ever had the burden of caring for a lawn, you'll be pleasantly surprised to find that flowers require much less attention than grass. Flower-garden maintenance can almost always wait until you have time for it.

Getting the Tools You Need

My garage is filled with gardening tools, but I find myself grabbing the same ones every time I head out the door. Start out with a few essentials, and you can always add to your supply later. (You don't actually need more tools than these essentials, but some folks are absolute tool nuts and can't resist collecting every new garden gadget on the market.)

Here's a list of the basic tools you need in order to work in your flower garden:

✔ **Buckets:** Buy several buckets. You need something to carry your small tools in as you work. A bucket is also perfect for mixing small amounts of soil and for carrying plants, trash, or weeds.

✔ **Hand trowel:** A hand trowel looks like a very small shovel. It's the tool you use the most in gardening, so buy a good one. A high-quality hand trowel costs as much as a shovel, but don't skimp. You use it to transplant small flowers and bulbs, to enlarge holes you've dug with a shovel, and to weed. You may want to buy two sizes — one with a wide blade for digging and one with a narrow blade for weeding. If you only buy one, get the wider size.

✔ **Pruning shears:** Dozens of types of pruning shears are available, but the two main classes are anvil and bypass. Get the bypass shears because they make cleaner cuts. These shears look and work much like snub-nosed scissors. They fit into tight spaces and cut cleanly.

Try out shears before you buy them to get a comfortable fit. Some stores keep twigs in their pruning-shear displays for just this purpose. When you hold the handles open in your hand, they shouldn't extend past the reach of your fingertips. Good pruning shears are very expensive, but they stay sharp longer than a cheap pair and have parts that are replaceable if they wear out.

✔ **Scissors:** A pair of lightweight aluminum household scissors are really slick for cutting foliage and lightweight stems (much larger handfuls than you can manage with pruning shears) and for all-around snipping. Scissors are also handy for cutting twine and opening bags (I can never get those stringed tops to unravel the way the directions say they do!).

✔ **Shovel or spade:** You need a shovel or spade for digging holes and for mixing amendments into the soil. I prefer a round-nose shovel, but many other gardeners swear by a short-handled, flat-bladed spade. Find a gardening friend who has both so that you can try them out before making your choice.

✔ **Stiff-tined rake:** A stiff-tined rake is helpful for smoothing out the surface of the soil and for spreading mulch. Use it with the tines up for spreading fine materials, tines down for coarse materials.

✔ **Watering can:** Use a watering can for spot-watering transplants and for mixing small batches of liquid fertilizer.

✔ **Wheelbarrow or garden cart:** Use a wheelbarrow or a garden cart (similar to a wheelbarrow but with two wheels) for carrying soil amendments, mulch, tools, and plants from the car to the flower bed. A wheelbarrow or garden cart is a real time- and back-saver. Buy one that you can handle easily.

Buying the right tools

Always buy the best quality tools you can afford. Cheap tools break too readily to be a true bargain. I've had countless trowels bend in half the first time they struck soil. Now I wouldn't accept a cheap trowel as a gift.

Don't order tools through the mail without first trying them out. One size doesn't fit all. You actually need to heft a tool to see whether you can use it comfortably. A bad fit guarantees backaches and blisters. After you know which tools suit your grip, go ahead and order them from a catalog, especially if you can save some money by doing so.

Small tools have a way of getting lost in the nooks and crannies of a flower bed. Two minutes after I set a trowel down, it vanishes. I swear they bury themselves. To make your tools easy to locate, paint a band of bright color or wrap a strip of colored tape on the part of the handle that you don't grab hold of. Some tools have a hole at one end so that you can hang them on a nail; tie a piece of brightly colored yarn through the hole to make your tool stand out against the garden's neutral backdrop. In this case, garish is good.

Good tools last a lifetime if you take care of them. Don't ever leave them outside where they can rust. Always quit gardening for the day while you still have enough energy and daylight to clean your tools and put them away.

Renting the really big puppies

Large, gasoline-powered machines are a real help with large projects, but they're expensive to buy and take up a great deal of storage space. Renting or borrowing these machines when you need them is more practical. Look in the Yellow Pages of your phone book for rental agencies. Usually, these machines are rented out by the hour or the day. Unless you have a hitch on your vehicle and a small trailer, expect to pay a delivery charge as well. Rental costs vary but are usually about the same as a moderately priced dinner. The two most useful large machines are power tillers and chipper-shredders:

✔ A *power tiller* is a mechanical soil mixer. It can make really light work of soil preparation, but after you dig your garden, you don't need to use a tiller again. Rather than buy your own, rent this big boy when needed.

✔ *Chipper-shredders* grind up twigs, branches, and other garden waste and can reduce a huge pile of such stuff to a small pile of chips and shreds. These little pieces rot much more quickly than unchopped material in the compost bin. Many communities no longer accept garden waste in the garbage pick-up, so you need to do something with it. You can either rent a chipper-shredder machine once a year, when you do a big cleanup, or hire a garden maintenance company to come in and grind the prunings for you.

Getting into a Maintenance Routine

Garden chores have several missions. Some are necessary mostly for the sake of tidiness. Others help preserve good garden health. Most gardeners fuss in their gardens much more than is necessary, just because playing in the garden is such an enjoyable and relaxing thing to do. A 100- to 200-square-foot (9- to 18-square-meter) flower garden shouldn't take more than a few minutes a week of tending, with a couple of hours of major cleanup several times a year. This section covers the housekeeping aspects of gardening, such as trimming, staking, and preparing your flower bed for winter. Watering (Chapter 8) and fertilizing (Chapter 9) are such important topics that they warrant their own chapters.

Deadheading

No, *deadheading* is not some kind of homage to Jerry Garcia. Flowers in a vase eventually start to wither and die, and so do flowers in the garden as they age. Removing these crumpled corpses serves several purposes:

✔ Dead flowers aren't very pretty. Cutting them off improves the look of the garden.

✔ Most dead flowers form seeds — which can be a good or a bad thing. Some plants replace flowers with really attractive seedheads. But others scatter their seeds all over the garden, much like a dandelion does. You often wind up with dozens of baby flowers that you have to pull out to avoid ending up with a hundred daisies in one square foot of garden soil. Cutting off flowers before they form seeds prevents this maintenance headache.

✔ Many perennials stop blooming after they form seeds, so removing the fading flowers before they can complete the process encourages the plant to continue blooming. Some perennials have their biggest burst of bloom in the spring but will rebloom in the fall if you cut off the first flush of flowers after they start to turn brown.

To deadhead, simply cut the dead flower off — using scissors for lightweight stems or pruning shears for heavy and thick ones. Cut the stem below the flower at the first leaves or flower bud you come to.

Disbudding

If you like your flowers really big, you may want to indulge in the practice of disbudding. Before the buds start to open, remove all but one or two flower buds on each stem. The plant then directs all its energy to the remaining buds, resulting in large flowers.

Gardeners commonly disbud dahlias, chrysanthemums, peonies, and carnations.

If you want more flowers rather than larger flowers, don't disbud. Every bud you remove is a flower you don't get to enjoy later.

The kindest cuts

Here are more things you can do with your pruning shears and scissors:

✔ **Pinching:** To keep perennials denser and shorter, you may want to pinch or shear them, as shown in Figure 10-1, a couple of times early in the season. This process is called pinching because you can actually pinch off the top of each stem between your thumb and forefinger — but using scissors or pruning shears is quicker and easier.

Figure 10-1: To keep late-flowering perennials more compact, shear or pinch a couple of times early in the season.

Simply snip (or pinch) off the top few inches (8 cm or so) of the plant when it grows to a foot tall (30 cm) in spring and again in the middle of summer. Every stem you cut grows several new stems. The result is stocky sprays of more, but smaller, flowers.

Chrysanthemums and asters are two perennials that are routinely pinched. Otherwise, they tend to get floppy.

✔ **Shearing:** For a quicker alternative to pinching, use scissors or pruning shears to cut the top 6 inches (15 cm) off your plants a couple of times before midsummer.

✔ **Cutting back hard:** When the directions for a plant tell you to cut it back hard, this means to reduce the height of the plant by approximately one-third to one-half. Use either scissors or pruning shears to cut the stems. Sometimes, this hard pruning is recommended solely to improve the appearance of the plant, but it may also be necessary to renew a plant's vigor.

Staking perennials with bad posture

Some perennials slouch and sprawl as badly as a group of teenage boys in the neighborhood park. If slumping perennials were simply a problem of aesthetics, you could just ignore them, depending on your inclination toward discipline in the garden. But when a large perennial leans over on top of smaller, weaker companions, the bully may steal all the sunlight or actually crush the little ones. During fall cleanup, you often find that plants subjected to this treatment didn't survive the season.

Fortunately, you have many ways to prop up unruly (or just plain lazy) plants. Figure 10-2 illustrates a few popular methods and devices for staking perennials:

✔ **Bamboo stakes:** Bamboo makes good support for flowers with tall, single spikes — such as delphiniums and lilies. Wait until the stems are several feet tall and starting to form flower buds. Pound the stake several inches into the ground at the base of the plant and tie the stem loosely to the stake. Use breadbag twist-ties, twine, or whatever you have on hand.

You can also encircle wide multistemmed perennials with bamboo-type stakes and run twine around the circumference and back and forth across the center a few times to make sort of a net — this way, the stems can grow through the twine and be supported.

✔ **Branches:** When you prune shrubs, save any trimmings that are 2 to 3 feet (60 cm to 1 m) and long and brushy at one end, resembling brooms. When a perennial reaches about a foot tall, poke several of these branches — bushy side up and leaning slightly inward — into the ground around the plant. The stems grow up through this circle of branches, while the supporting mechanism is hidden by the foliage of the perennial.

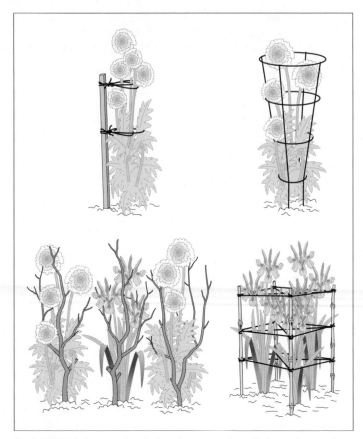

Figure 10-2: A few popular devices for preventing tall, floppy flowers from falling on their faces.

Branches are also the best form of remedial support after your poor perennial has fallen flat on its face. Have someone gather up the sprawling stems while you shove a branch underneath, bushy side up, to hold the stems up. Using branches in this way isn't a perfect solution, but it's better than nothing.

✔ **Commercial supports:** You can buy artistic metal supports from garden centers and nursery catalogs. The wire cages I use for my tomato and peony plants are at the low end of the market. Also available are wrought-iron stakes and collapsible frame types.

A born-again staker

I used to be anti-staking. Many garden writers suggest planting your perennials tightly together so that they hold one another upright. This advice appears to be sensible and less work — and I always opt for less work. But this strategy hasn't worked for me. My perennials are packed together as densely as carpet pile, but several still manage to flop over and do a great deal of damage, in spite of their crowded conditions.

Staking after the flop is much harder than staking beforehand, so, every year, the list of perennials I stake grows longer. I use commercial tomato and peony cages — contraptions made of wire rings and legs. They're inexpensive and easy to install. You just push them into the soil so that they surround the perennial as it emerges in the spring. In the fall, the cages go back into the garage for storage.

Curing overpopulation woes

Overplanting initially is easy. Everyone does it. Envisioning the space that a full-grown peony needs is difficult even for the most cautious among us. Besides, the perennials don't read descriptions of themselves, and they don't always stop growing when they reach the allotted width. Many continue to widen indefinitely, until they hit a physical barrier that stops them. During the first few years, you're certain your garden is never going to fill in. But by the third or fourth year, you have more flowers than you know what to do with.

Many perennials also spread by seed. Even if you deadhead scrupulously, a few flowers inevitably form a few seeds, which then germinate. You may be greeted one spring by dozens of Shasta daisies where you had planted three the previous year. To restore some order, you need to occasionally intervene. Otherwise, after several years the pushiest perennials are the only ones left in the flower bed. Weaker flowers have been overrun by the advancing hordes.

Spring and fall are good times to look things over with a critical eye. Yank out seedlings as they come up in crowded areas. If you decide to leave a few seedlings to fill a bare spot, thin them to at least one foot (30 cm) apart. Put a stick next to the ones you plan to keep and pull out all the others. (You can replant seedlings in other parts of the garden, give them away to friends and neighbors, or compost them.) When clumps of flowers outgrow their space, dig up the whole bunch and divide them.

A Schedule of Chores

The easiest way to see that necessary chores get done in a somewhat timely fashion is to set up some sort of schedule. Don't fret if you're out of town for a couple of weeks; the flower garden can wait until you get back without getting too impatient.

Weekly work

Take a few minutes each day to walk outside and have a look at your flower bed — just for the sheer heck of it. At least once a week, take along a bucket with a hand trowel, scissors, and pruning shears and spend a few minutes tidying up. These are some of the things you should do:

- Cut off dead or dying flowers or leaves.
- Pull any weeds you find.
- Toss straying mulch back into the flower bed (for more about mulch, see Chapter 11).
- Squash any bad bugs you can catch (to recognize the good, the bad, and the ugly bugs, turn to Chapter 12).
- Stake any flowers that look as though they may topple over.
- Treat plagues of bugs or diseases that have appeared during the past week (see Chapter 12).
- Water as necessary. (See Chapter 8 to help you decide when necessary is.)

Monthly maintenance

In addition to your weekly gardening chores, other jobs need attention about once a month. You can work these tasks into your weekly routine, allowing yourself a little extra time once a month.

✔ Adjust your watering as the weather changes. Give your flower bed more water during hot weather, less during cool weather.

✔ As each perennial stops blooming, cut it back by about a third. Or, if you want, you can cut the old stalks to the ground after new leaves start to sprout from the base of the plant, for the sake of appearance. It's your call.

✔ Make notes in your diary of both artistic and practical successes and failures — "The daisy and the ornamental grasses are pretty together" or "The neighbor's cat ate the catmint," and so on.

Springtime strategy

Spring is the busiest time in the garden in most regions. As the weather starts to warm up, funnel some of your spring-fever energy into garden chores:

✔ In cold-winter and cool-summer climates, spring is the best time to plant perennials in your flower bed (see Chapter 7).

✔ Renew your mulch by adding a few inches of fresh material, if the old material is getting thin (see Chapter 11).

✔ Plant summer bulbs.

✔ In cold-winter climates, plant annuals.

✔ Fertilize the flower bed (see Chapter 9).

Autumn action

Fall is the second busiest season in the garden. After a long summer of sipping lemonade and admiring your garden handiwork, you need to devote a short burst of activity to your garden before winter sets in:

✔ In hot-summer, warm-winter climates, plant perennials in the fall (see Chapter 7).

✔ Plant spring bulbs.

✔ Prepare flower beds for planting the following spring (see Chapter 6).

✔ You may want to build other structures — such as trellises, walls, paths, and so on — in the fall, while the weather is cool.

✔ In warm-winter climates, plant annuals.

Putting the garden to bed for winter

If you live in a warm-winter climate, you can skip this section. All you need to do is clean up year-round, whenever your flowers show signs of wear — cutting off dead flowers, leaves, and stems as they materialize.

However, if frosts and snows are an annual feature of your backyard, the onset of winter is the time to do a few things to protect your plants:

✔ Water less frequently. For example, if you've been watering twice a week, switch to once a week. Cutting down on water helps signal to the plants that they need to toughen up and hunker down for winter.

✔ Dig and store tender bulbs after the first frost has blackened the foliage.

✔ Replace mulch from under any perennials that were besieged by insects during the growing season. Getting rid of the mulch also gets rid of any eggs. You can safely compost the old mulch.

✔ Place a 4- to 6-inch (10- to 15-cm) layer of organic mulch around perennials that you planted in late summer and fall, if you haven't done so already (see Chapter 11). You can also let leaves that fall into the flower bed stay where they land to add to the mulch layer.

✔ Cut back the stems on perennials (at least the ones that don't have pretty seedheads) to within 8 to 10 inches (20 to 26 cm) of the ground. In really severe winter climates — where the temperature is often below 0° F (–18° C), don't cut back your perennials until late winter or early spring. The debris helps protect them from the cold.

✔ After the ground freezes (or in midwinter if the ground doesn't freeze), cover your whole flower bed with a loose mulch of hay, straw, or evergreen boughs. This extra layer protects your fragile perennials from severe cold. Leave this mulch in place until early spring and then remove it gradually as the weather starts to warm up.

✔ In dry-winter climates, water the flower bed once a month whenever snow or rain hasn't fallen in recent memory. Water on a warm, sunny day so that the water can soak into the ground (see Chapter 8).

Whenever an unseasonable frost is forecast, you can save your flowers by covering them with old sheets or special frost blankets, as shown in Figure 10-3. (Don't cover your flowers with plastic; it conducts cold too readily.) Leave the sheets or frost blankets in place until the cold snap is over. Cold-weather gardeners always need a few lengths of frost blanket, which is available from garden centers. This magical material is fairly expensive, but it lasts many years if dried between uses and stored out of direct sunlight.

If you live in a cold-winter climate, don't fertilize your plants after midsummer. Fertilizer encourages plants to put on soft new growth, which is really vulnerable to frost damage.

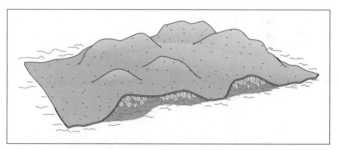

Figure 10-3: For temporary protection from severe cold, cover your perennials with frost blankets.

Chapter 11

Mulching Around

*M*ulch is a layer of material spread over the surface of the soil between the plants in the garden. Almost any material works; shredded polyester leisure suits do just fine, if you've got a closet full of them that you can't get rid of at garage sales. In fact, vegetable gardeners are much more practical and less concerned about aesthetics than flower gardeners, and they use some pretty odd stuff for mulch — such as old carpet strips.

Nature provides a great model for mulching. Trees create their own mulch by dropping an accumulation of leaf litter on the forest floor. Even in dry regions, undisturbed soil is generally covered by broken rock or gravel.

What Mulch Can Do for You

You may balk at paying good money for a material that resembles a mix of twigs and sweepings from the workshop floor. But mulch pays for itself by reducing water bills and fertilizer needs, not to mention fostering an overall healthier garden.

Any mulch, regardless of what it's made of, acts as a protective covering to the soil and benefits your garden in a number of ways.

- **Controlling weeds:** Because bare earth is an invitation that no self-respecting weed can ignore for long, mulch is the garden's no-vacancy sign. The few weeds that manage to germinate (sprout and begin to grow) in organic mulch come up elongated and are easy to pull out. Rock mulches aren't really as effective at discouraging weeds as the organics, so you must be more vigilant about weeding a flowerbed with rock mulch in it.

- **Preventing soil erosion:** Heavy drops of water from rainfall or sprinklers smash into the surface of unprotected soil and break a good soil's crumblike texture into very small particles. These tiny particles form a crust that facilitates runoff and soil erosion. When water hits the nooks and crannies of a mulched surface, however, it gets trapped until it trickles down into the soil underneath — right where you want it to go.

- **Making your garden pretty:** Spreading mulch between your flowers gives your garden a unified, finished appearance, especially if you use the same mulch throughout your landscape. Some types of mulch are really quite attractive in their own right. The edges of the flowerbeds act as a frame for your perennials, and mulch is the matting.

- **Slowing evaporation:** Mulch helps the soil in your garden retain moisture by shading it from the full blast of the sun and wind, measurably reducing evaporation (losing moisture to the air). Using mulch nearly always results in lower water bills. Plus, you don't need to water as often — a real time-saver if you don't have an automatic irrigation system.

- **Preventing temperature swings:** Mulch protects perennials from sudden changes in air temperature, allowing a more gradual warm-up as temperatures rise during the heat of the day, and a corresponding slower cool-down at night. In climates that experience wide seasonal swings of hot and cold, mulch creates an insulating blanket that gives the plants more time to adjust to the change of seasons.

The effects of mulch on self-sowing seeds

Many types of organic mulches contain naturally-occurring chemicals that retard seed germination, which is the very reason that they are so effective for weed control. However, not many flower seeds germinate in these mulches either. This lack of germination can be a good thing for discouraging weeds, but if you're hoping for the serendipity of randomly self-sowing flower seedlings, you may be disappointed.

On the other hand, most seeds that land in gravel germinate readily. You may want to factor the extra maintenance of removing unwanted seedlings into the decision of whether or not to use a rock mulch.

Choosing the Best Mulch for Your Garden

Before deciding which kind of mulch is the best choice for your garden, you need to be aware of some very real differences among the various types of mulch. The three basic kinds of mulch are

- ✓ **Organics:** Derived from living plant residues, organic mulches are readily available in diverse forms as byproducts of the agriculture, timber, and horticulture industries.

- ✓ **Inorganics:** Various rock products, including gravel, stone chips, river rock, and lava rock (scorea), serve as inorganic mulch.

- ✓ **Weed control barriers:** Weed control barriers can be organic or inorganic, such as newspaper, or woven fabric. These barriers are best used along with a layer of an organic or inorganic mulch.

No one mulch is perfect for every situation. But keep in mind that choosing the wrong mulch is not a disaster — only a potential inconvenience. You can always take it off and try something else.

Going organic

One of the prime benefits of an organic mulch is that it gradually decomposes, and the resulting decayed matter works its way down into the soil. Teeming communities of insects and microorganisms thrive in the cool, moist shelter of a rotting mulch. As they digest the mulch, they release a steady, slow supply of nutrients. You get on-going passive soil amendment — without the back-wrenching digging. (For more on soil amendment, refer to Chapter 6.)

Pull back the leaf litter in a woodland, and you notice that the soil beneath resembles large crumbs. Decaying organic matter releases chemicals that cause small soil particles to clump together, helping to improve the soil's texture and health. This decaying process is especially important in perennial flower gardens, where you amend the soil only once and then leave it undisturbed for many years or perhaps a lifetime. No one-time soil amendment can be expected to last that long.

You need to replenish the top of the mulch as the bottom decays. How often you need to put down more mulch depends on where you live and the type of organic material you use. In wet climates, decomposition can be very quick. In drier areas, the same material may last several years. Small particles generally break down faster than large ones, and products containing a large percentage of wood decompose faster than bark. Water, heat, and fertilizer all accelerate the decaying process.

Here are some other factors to consider when choosing a mulch:

- ✔ **Flammability:** Recent social trends have created a new mulch hazard. When smokers go outside for breaks, dropped matches or cigarettes can ignite some organic mulches. Areas around public buildings are more at risk than areas around private residences, but be careful just the same, especially in fire-prone areas. Pine needles, recycled wood mulches, hay, and straw can all increase fire danger.

- ✔ **Nitrogen depletion:** Nitrogen depletion is the loss of nitrogen, an essential nutrient, from the soil. This problem is most likely to occur when you use finely chipped, woody mulches — sawdust is the classic example.

Microorganisms that decompose the sawdust consume all the available nitrogen in the soil, depriving your perennials of the nitrogen they need. Plants that aren't getting enough nitrogen become stunted and chlorotic, or yellow-looking.

If a large percentage of plants in your garden show these symptoms, or if you want to prevent nitrogen depletion, add 2 pounds (1 kg) of complete fertilizer (look for at least 10-10-10) per 100 square feet (9 sq. m). Spread this fertilizer over the soil before putting down the mulch or scatter it on top of an existing mulch.

✔ **Wet, low-lying areas:** Take care when using organic mulches in low, poorly drained areas where water collects. The decomposition that occurs in wet areas produces chemicals that are toxic to perennials. You don't want to make a wet spot even wetter, and mulch slows down the drying process.

Let's rock

Organic mulches help make the soil ideal for a wide variety of perennials, particularly perennials native to meadows and woodlands. But when growing xeric plants (plants from dry regions), the same conditions can actually damage plants, especially when you're trying to grow them in soggier climates. Plants from arid regions evolved in an environment that is radically different from what traditional perennials enjoy. Soils in these areas are high in mineral content, low in organic matter and microorganisms, and strewn with a covering of rock chips (if covered with anything at all).

Most dryland perennials can't cope with the large numbers of fungi and bacteria present in rich garden soils and can be very susceptible to damage caused by these organisms. Plants that don't succumb to disease sometimes grow themselves to death due to the abundant soil nutrients. They may become overly large and floppy or set seed and die quickly — essentially adopting the life cycle of an annual. Such plants are healthier and longer-lived when treated to a rock mulch that more closely resembles their natural conditions.

Several inches of gravel or rock chips hold the crown of the plant above the soil surface and improve up drainage while doing all those other things that a mulch does — holding moisture in the root zone and insulating the soil to maintain a more constant temperature.

Ultimately, the decision whether to choose an organic or a rock mulch usually comes down to what you like best. Most gardeners have strong preferences toward one or the other, and most plants adapt to either one.

Using weed barriers

Plastic films, landscaping fabric, newspaper, cardboard, old carpet, and roofing paper are all excellent materials for underlaying walks and placing between rows of a vegetable garden. These barriers are highly effective at preventing weed growth and can be used where low maintenance is a primary goal and a regimented look is acceptable.

Don't use clear or black plastic films or other nonporous materials on perennial gardens except during bed preparation. They block water and air exchange in the soil and can cause your perennials to rot.

To install weed barriers, follow these steps:

1. **Roll the weed barrier out over the prepared soil, overlapping the seams generously.**

2. **Fasten the material in place with landscape pins.**

   You can use pieces of wire or coat hangers, bent into a U-shape, in place of landscape pins.

3. **Cut holes (with scissors) for your perennials and then plant them through the openings.**

   Use care not to scatter soil on top of the fabric, because weeds will happily establish themselves there.

4. **Finally, spread a layer of an organic or rock mulch to a depth of 2 to 3 inches (5 to 8 cm) on top of the fabric.**

   This mulch layer protects the material from UV light, lends a more traditional appearance to the finished bed, and also holds the lightweight material in place.

Landscape fabrics have some drawbacks and cautions for use:

✔ Don't use weed barriers at the bottom of slopes, where soil can wash down from above.

✔ Avoid covering landscape fabrics with organic mulches composed of small particles that may decay quickly.

Washed-down soil and decayed organic mulch both create excellent conditions for weeds to sprout. Weed seeds generally germinate from above, sending their roots downward through the fabric into the earth below. When weeds do take hold, their roots can become thoroughly enmeshed in the fabric's fibers. The weeds are almost impossible to pull out without tearing the fabric badly.

✔ A more critical problem with these types of barriers is that the soil is kept out of contact with the mulch, which means that you lose the benefit of passive soil amendment.

✔ A flower bed prepared in this manner is not very flexible. Every time you want to move or add a perennial, you must cut another hole, and more holes mean more opportunities for weeds to grow.

Rock or chunky mulches are the best mulches for suppressing weeds when used in combination with weed barriers.

It's Mulching Time

Timing is critical when laying down mulch. Weed seeds germinate readily in a newly prepared flower bed, so you need to apply mulch as soon as possible after planting. The optimal depth of the mulch varies, depending on which type of mulch you use and the character of your soil. As a general rule, use only enough mulch to completely cover the surface of the soil. Use more on sandy soils and less on clay. Guidelines for depth and coverage are

✔ 1 to 2 inches (2.5 to 5 cm) of very fine materials (for example, compost or buckwheat hulls)

✔ 2 to 3 inches (5 to 8 cm) of coarser materials (for example, shredded wood or bark)

↙ 3 to 4 inches (8 to 10 cm) of loose materials (for example, hay, straw, or pine needles)

One cubic yard covers a 10 x 12-foot (120 sq. ft.) area to a depth of 1 to 2 inches. (One cubic meter covers a 3 x 4-meter or 12 sq. meter area to a depth of 2 to 5 cm.) See the Quick Reference Card in the front of this book for additional coverage rates.

The following are step-by-step instructions for applying mulch:

1. **Spread the mulch between the plants to an even depth.**

   A three-pronged tiller is handy for smoothing the mulch out.

2. **Keep organics away from the crown of each perennial.**

3. **Leave a shallow crater around each perennial (see Figure 11-1).**

4. **After applying the mulch, water thoroughly.**

   Wet the mulch so that it doesn't pull moisture from the soil or blow away.

Figure 11-1: When spreading mulch, always leave a crater around each perennial.

Avoiding the Mulch Uglies

Sometimes, you learn the hard way. I built a path on the side of the house and mulched it heavily with several inches of small bark chunks. Within a month, a single, strong storm blew all that expensive bark away, presumably to Oz. Chagrined, I swept up what little was left and replaced it with heavy river cobble, hoping that it was heavy enough to withstand the next strong wind. I'm happy to report that the river cobble has stayed put!

Keeping mulch in its place

The greatest difficulty with lightweight organic mulches is keeping them in place. Mulch tends to suffer from wanderlust. What doesn't blow away often floats off instead. Every time we have a real gully-washer, all the chunk bark in the entire neighborhood washes away into the storm drains. Hillsides present an even worse problem, because gravity causes many materials to tumble down the slope. Solutions that use chicken wire, plastic mesh, or inverted wire U's are not very conducive to flower gardening. Shredded or fibrous organic mulches mat down and stay in place better than fine compost or bark nuggets. Gravel and rock chips work better yet. Larger rock, such as 4- to 6-inch (10- to 15-cm) river stones, withstand almost any force of nature.

Mulch scattered onto sidewalks, patios, driveways, and lawns is a real nuisance. You can corral the mulch by digging the level of the flower bed several inches lower than surrounding areas. Or dig a trench approximately one foot wide and several inches deep alongside the edge of the flowerbeds to trap mulch that falls, like the one shown in Figure 11-2. As the trench fills with mulch, simply toss it back onto the flower bed as part of routine maintenance.

Figure 11-2: Dig a trench alongside pavement to catch falling mulch.

Keeping out the debris

When tree leaves, twigs, and other garden litter fall into an organic mulch, they can be left to be absorbed into the mulch. With a rock mulch, anything that lands on it immediately looks messy. (I watched in utter amazement as one of the major thoroughfares near my home was shut down for a week one summer so that work crews could wash the cobble mulch in the center median with high power hoses!) Never use rock mulch at the bottom of a hillside, where soil or organic mulch from above can easily wash down onto it. A power leaf blower does a respectable job of cleaning rock mulch, but take care to use the blower when the flowerbed is dormant in order to prevent plant injury.

Don't mix mulches

Another common problem with mulches is using two incompatible types where they can intermingle. Organics and rocks don't combine attractively, and few people have the patience to separate the two. Choose one or the other for the whole bed. You can safely use different mulches in non-adjoining flower beds to accommodate more than one plant community's needs — but use a barrier in between. The wider the barrier, the more effective it is. For example, an expanse of lawn or a brick walk always works better than a strip of metal edging.

Layering different types of organic materials on top of one another is fine, because they all eventually weather to a uniform brownish gray. For economy, place a free or inexpensive mulch underneath a thin layer of a more costly product, such as shredded cedar or redwood. Add more of the attractive mulch whenever necessary to keep the color looking fresh. Different rock types don't blend well, but for a more natural look, you can mix several sizes of the same type of rock.

 Always check out the neighbor's landscape before putting a flower bed on the property line. Coordinate with any mulch on the other side for ease of maintenance. If the existing mulch is too weird for you (you don't like white marble chips, for example), you may want to rethink the placement of your flower bed. If anything is worse than white marble chips, it's white marble chips decorated with your cedar bark!

Creatures in the Mulch

A wide range of critters — some beneficial, others not so welcome — make their home in the cool, moist shelter of an organic mulch. When you spread organic mulch, expect to see increases in the numbers of wood-eating and wood-inhabiting insects as well as pillbugs, earwigs, millipedes, and centipedes. Most mulch inhabitants are harmless to living plants, and some of them prey upon one another, helping to keep things under control.

Molds and fungi

With the increased use of recycled wood products, some really interesting organisms are becoming more prevalent.

✔ One mulch invader that always gets a reaction is *slime mold* — a yellow, frothy growth that looks very much as though the dog's been sick in the garden. But don't be alarmed — these curiosities are completely harmless to plants, pets, and humans. They just eat the mulch.

✔ Another oddity that you may run into is *bird's nest fungus.* This growth usually appears in organic mulches that have been down for two or three years. This harmless fungus consists of tiny, cup-shaped bodies that are filled with egg-shaped, spore-filled sacs.

✔ *Artillery fungus* can be a serious annoyance to the fastidious. It shoots spores up to twenty feet and targets light-colored surfaces. When these spore masses stick to house walls, as they often do, the black dots look like fly specks and are almost impossible to scrub off.

Although you can ignore all these growths (or use them as conversation starters), prevention strategies do exist. Because most of these growths develop in cool, damp weather, raking or cultivating the mulch during periods of such weather interrupts their spread. Or you can switch to (or top-dress with) a layer of cedar or redwood products. Both contain natural fungal inhibitors. If all else fails, eliminate their food source by removing the mulch.

Perennial pests

Insect pests and diseases that attack the same perennials year after year can take up residence and spend the winter in the organic mulch underneath the plant. Because most problems are host-specific (meaning that they attack only one species or family of plants), you can break the cycle by thoroughly cleaning out the mulch from around any plant that's under siege. Compost the old mulch or move it to another section of the garden (most pests can't easily make their way back). Then replenish the mulch with fresh, new material that's free of pests and their eggs. (If insects or diseases are a problem in your flowerbed, turn — without delay — to Chapter 12.)

Chapter 12

Trouble in Paradise

· ·

· ·

I am going to let you in on one of gardening's dirty little secrets: You can ignore most of the bugs that visit your garden.

Folks that make and sell bug-killing products may try to convince you otherwise, but don't believe them. Doing nothing at all about bugs is often the best policy. Ninety-five percent of the bugs that visit your garden are either beneficial or neutral — neither good nor bad. But ignoring even the genuine pests gives nature's own controls the time they need to kick in. In most cases, nature's way is a much better remedy than anything you can buy.

A Plan of Action

You can make your garden as sterile as ground zero of a nuclear blast site if you use enough poison. But doing so isn't a very practical goal, and sterile conditions don't make for very satisfying gardens, either. If you enjoy butterflies, you must be prepared to put up with their caterpillars eating the leaves of your flowers. No caterpillars, no butterflies! Similarly, songbirds don't stick around long if your garden has no bugs for them to eat.

The key is to strike a balance — tolerating some damage to accommodate the needs of wildlife that you want to attract, but acting quickly when outbreaks of harmful insects or disease threaten to get out of control.

An ounce of prevention

Preventing a problem is easier than treating its results. Here are some things you can do to head off disasters before they strike:

- Keep your flowers healthy and strong. Just as you are more susceptible to the flu when you're run down, opportunistic bugs and diseases move in for the kill when flowers are weakened by improper growing conditions. Placing flowers where their sun, soil, water, and fertilizer requirements are met helps them fend off these attacks.

- Practice good housekeeping habits in your garden. Remove dead and diseased leaves and stems promptly to get diseases out of the garden before they spread. Keep the flowerbed clear of weeds that can play host to diseases or insects. Clean and disinfect pruning shears and scissors (dip them in a solution of household bleach and water) after cutting diseased plants. If you smoke, wash your hands before gardening — tobacco can contain viruses that infect flowers.

- Shower your flowers. If you use drip-type irrigation, occasionally wash the dust and small insects off your flowers by using a spray attachment on the end of a hose. Get up underneath the leaves to knock off bugs that are clinging there.

  Spray your garden in the morning so that the foliage dries quickly, especially in hot, humid weather. Continually wet leaves promote some diseases.

- Provide good air circulation. If you have disease problems, give the plants more space. Diseases spread more quickly when plants touch.

- Don't bring bugs or diseases into your garden. When you buy new plants, check them over carefully to make sure that insects or their eggs aren't lurking on the undersides of the leaves. Don't buy plants with mottled, discolored, or spotted foliage. Look for pearly clumps of snail or slug eggs when you remove your flower from its pot, and destroy any that you find. Pull off any weeds that are hitchhiking with your flower before you plant it in your garden.

✔ Encourage natural helpers. Learn to ignore the good guys (even the creepy ones), and they'll do much of your work for you. Snakes eat slugs and mice. Bats, spiders, toads, and lizards all eat huge quantities of bugs, if you let them.

✔ Get rid of problem plants. Be hard-hearted and replace any flower that's a perennial problem. Too many healthy choices are available for you to put up with disease and bug magnets.

Playing detective

Spotting damage on the perennials that you're working so hard to grow can be frustrating, but don't overreact. Perennials are a tough bunch. A few holes in their leaves don't damage their vigor and probably aren't noticeable at ten paces anyway.

If you're using insecticide to control bug damage, you may actually be aggravating the problem. For example, spraying insecticides indiscriminately can kill the insects that normally eat spider mites, resulting in a population explosion of the mites. (Some insecticides don't kill the mites because mites aren't true insects.)

Before you get involved in chemical warfare, find out exactly what's causing the problem. Environmental damage often creates symptoms that look very much like disease or insect mischief. Ask yourself whether any of the following conditions may be responsible for your flowers' ill health.

✔ **Air pollution:** Some flowers are sensitive to smog. Their leaves may appear bleached or distorted. If air pollution is your problem, ask a local nursery person to recommend smog resistant varieties.

✔ **Chemical damage:** Symptoms of chemical damage include distorted and twisted stems and foliage, browning in an even pattern over the whole plant, or irregularly-shaped brown spots. If you use herbicides, do so on cool, still days to prevent spray from accidentally drifting or descending as a vapor cloud onto your flower beds. Swimming pool chemicals can also damage plants. Mix all chemicals away from the flower bed and immediately put the lid back on the container to limit vapors from escaping.

- ✔ **Drought:** Too little water causes plants to become warped-looking, stop growing, and develop brown tips or yellowing leaves.

- ✔ **Fertilizer burn:** Applying fertilizer improperly can scorch plant leaves. Too much can actually kill the plant.

- ✔ **Fertilizer deficiency:** Shortages of any of the essential plant nutrients can cause stunting and leaf discoloration.

- ✔ **Freeze damage:** Frost can either blacken the most exposed parts of the plant or kill the plant to the ground. Hardy perennials usually grow back after freeze damage, but, just to be safe, protect plants from unseasonable cold spells by temporarily covering them with old sheets or blankets. Don't use plastic — frost goes right through plastic.

- ✔ **Inadequate sunlight:** When a flower isn't getting enough light, it turns sickly pale and its stems become long and spindly. If you plant in a shady area, choose shade-tolerant flowers. (See Chapter 5 for a list of shade-tolerant perennials.)

- ✔ **Poor drainage:** Flowers that are too wet become yellowish or brown, wilt, and eventually die. Plant flowers that are tolerant of wet conditions or improve the drainage in your flower bed.

- ✔ **Salts:** Salt can either occur naturally in the soil or get carried to your garden on salt-ridden breezes, if you live near the ocean. Cars can also splash salt onto your garden when roads are salted in the winter. When salt concentrations build up, your flowers can become stunted and brown. The cure is to rinse the soil with plenty of fresh water.

- ✔ **Sunscald:** When shade-loving flowers are getting too much sunshine, they first become pale all over and then may develop papery patches or dark, irregular burns. Move the plant to a shadier location.

- ✔ **Transplant shock:** A recently moved flower can go into a real sulk and wilt badly. Provide temporary shelter from the sun and wind until the plant recovers and has settled into its new home.

If you're certain that a pest is responsible for your flower damage, you need to clearly identify which insect is the guilty party. Don't jump to conclusions. Consider a damaged plant covered with both aphids and ladybugs. Without your glasses, you may not be able to see the tiny aphids, so you may assume that the ladybugs are eating your flowers. Actually, the ladybugs are dining on the aphids, who are the real culprits! Use a magnifying glass to look for wee pests.

A marauder's row of insects

If you think that insects are eating your flowers, the first thing you need to do is identify the suspects. Then you can decide how to best rid your garden of them. Don't panic when you look over the following list. Most insect infestations are localized — you aren't likely to ever get to know all these pests, unless you move around quite a bit. Insects also have good and bad seasons. You may be thoroughly plagued by leafhoppers one year but not find a single one the next.

The following list describes the most common insect pests of perennial gardens and how to get rid of them. If you can't identify the bugs in your garden, take one on a field trip to a local nursery or see whether your local library has a book with photos of garden pests.

- ✓ **Aphids:** Often the first indication of aphid infestation is an odd twisting and distortion of the foliage. A close-up look reveals crowds of pear-shaped little bugs, which suck plant sap with their needlelike noses (see Figure 12-1). Some aphids are wingless; others have wings. Aphids come in a rainbow of colors. Wash them off with a spray of water or use insecticidal soap.

- ✓ **Beetles:** Many types of beetles eat perennials; many other types eat bugs. If you catch them in the act, you can tell the difference. Otherwise, capture one and take it into a nursery or your local cooperative extension office to find out whether yours is a good beetle or a bad beetle. My policy is to ignore the odd beetle and only take notice if hordes of them appear. Knock slow-moving beetles into a bucket of water, hand-pick and smash them, or spray them with *neem, rotenone,* or *sabadilla* (these are relatively safe plant-derived insecticides that you can buy at any garden center). Figure 12-2 shows an up-close-and-personal view of a Japanese beetle.

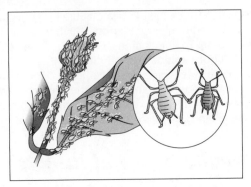

Figure 12-1: Aphids are a common garden pest.

Figure 12-2: The Japanese beetle is a common pest in many regions.

✔ **Caterpillars:** *Caterpillars* are the larvae of moths and butterflies. Usually, butterfly caterpillars are big, brightly colored, and travel alone. You may decide to look the other way when one of these critters inches by. Other types run in packs and do a great deal of damage munching on leaves and flower buds. Still another type of caterpillar, called *borers,* tunnel destructively through stems or roots.

Cutworms (pictured in Figure 12-3) are soil-dwelling caterpillars who cut off whole young plants at ground level. Hand-pick and cut these invaders in half with scissors. Alternatively, you may spray them with Bt (Bacillus thuringiensis, the fancy name for a bacterial disease that infects caterpillars). Be aware, though, that Bt dispatches the butterfly caterpillars just as efficiently as the caterpillars you don't want.

Figure 12-3: Cutworms are a common pest of young plants.

- ✔ **Leafhoppers:** Little wedge-shaped leafhoppers suck plant juices but don't do much damage themselves. However, these insect Typhoid Marys carry a disease called *aster yellows,* which does particularly nasty things to flowers. When the leafhoppers appear in swarms, spray them with neem or rotenone.

- ✔ **Leaf miners:** Leaf miners are tiny fly maggots that tunnel in leaves, resulting in tell-tale trails (see Figure 12-4). Remove infected leaves and dispose of them — bugs and all. Or spray the whole plant with neem or a summer horticultural spray oil.

Figure 12-4: You can spot leaf miners by the trails they leave.

- ✔ **Mealybugs:** Furry little white oval-shaped critters, mealybugs would be cute if they didn't do so much damage and multiply so rapidly. Spray them with insecticidal soap, neem, or summer horticultural spray oil. (See mealybugs in Figure 12-5.)

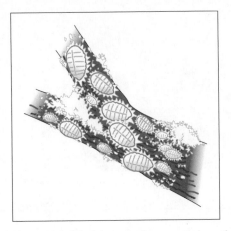

Figure 12-5: Mealybugs don't move much, so they're easy to spot.

✔ **Spider mites:** As their name implies, spider mites are actually tiny arachnids, not true insects. Usually, the first hint of a spider mite invasion is a mottled bronze tint to the foliage. A closer look reveals minute, traveling dots about the size of the period at the end of this sentence (see Figure 12-6). Wash the spiders off with a strong spray of water or spray them with insecticidal soap, sulfur, or summer horticultural spray oil (available at your local garden center).

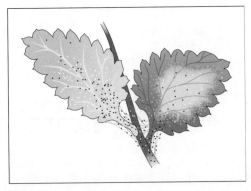

Figure 12-6: Individual spider mites are tiny, but the damage caused by hundreds is easy to spot.

✔ **Thrips:** If your flowers turn brown and are distorted and streaked with silver, tiny thrips are the culprit. Cut off and dispose of the infested buds. Knock the bugs off with a strong spray of water or spray them with an insecticidal soap, summer horticultural spray oil, or neem.

✔ **Weevils:** Beetles with long snouts are called weevils. They often drill holes in flower buds so the flowers don't open properly, if at all. Hand-pick and destroy them or spray with neem.

✔ **Whiteflies:** Small, snow-white whiteflies suck plant juices and reproduce at lightning speed. Symptoms of whitefly attack are mottled and yellowed leaves. Spray infested leaves with insecticidal soap, summer horticultural spray oil, or neem. Figure 12-7 shows a leaf infested with whiteflies.

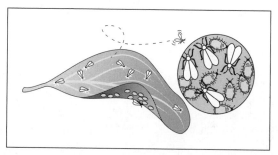

Figure 12-7: Whiteflies suck plant juices.

Playing Doctor with Plant Diseases

You may be surprised to learn that plants can get sick by their own versions of the same organisms that attack you and me — fungi, bacteria, viruses, and microplasma. Although flowers can't go to the doctor when they get sick or get vaccinations to prevent disease, you can do plenty to limit the spread of diseases in your flower bed.

Using insecticides

Before you purchase an insecticide, be sure to accurately identify the pest. Most insecticides don't kill all insects. Some bugs are resistant or immune to certain insecticides, so you need to be sure that the product you buy kills the bug you're hunting.

Applying a product that doesn't kill the beasts that are eating your flowers is a waste of time and money and can be harmful to the environment. Read the label to make sure that your target bug is listed.

To use insecticides wisely and safely, follow these precautions:

- ✔ Use insecticides as a last resort. You can control many outbreaks of small insects by simply washing them off the flowers with a strong spray from a hose.

- ✔ Use the least poisonous product that does the job. All the recom-

mendations in this chapter are relatively safe products that don't leave dangerous chemical residues in your garden, but you must be careful with any insecticide.

- ✔ Read the label carefully and thoroughly. Don't guess at how much insecticide to use or when or how to apply the product. Every insecticide has a unique set of instructions. The label tells you exactly how to use the product correctly and safely.

- ✔ Wear protective clothing. Cover up bare skin — wear long-sleeved clothing, rubber gloves, a nose/mouth mask, and goggles.

- ✔ Spray the undersides of leaves. Most insects and their eggs hide underneath leaves. Aim for a direct hit for better results.

 Plants are much more susceptible to disease when they're tired. Keep your flowers growing strong and, most important, don't overwater. Plant diseases are primarily water-borne. Letting the soil dry out between waterings is the simplest way to slow down their spread.

- ✔ **Aster yellows:** Aster yellows would be thoroughly entertaining if it didn't do so much damage. Plants infected with this disease become bizarrely deformed and distorted — the flowers may start to grow strange protrusions and the leaves curl and twist. Aster yellows is spread only by leafhoppers (an insect described in the preceding section). Pull and dispose of diseased plants.

✔ **Gray molds:** Ever-present fungi grow on dead plant tissue, but when conditions are to their liking, molds sometimes invade healthy plants. Fuzzy brown or gray mold forms on leaves and flowers, and stems may become soft and rotten. Cool temperatures and humidity encourage their growth. Where this disease is a problem, water in the morning so that plants dry quickly. Remove damaged leaves and flowers and destroy badly affected plants. To prevent mold, space flowers in the garden widely enough that they don't touch and clean up dead plant debris promptly.

✔ **Leafspots:** Brown or black irregular blotches or circular spots can be caused by both viral and bacterial infections. Remove leaves with these symptoms; simply removing the infected leaves may be enough to stop the spread of the infection. Destroy badly infected plants. Water early in the day so that foliage can dry out.

✔ **Nematodes:** Nematodes are actually microscopic worms that can damage plant roots or foliage. Root nematodes live in moist, sandy soils. Adding large quantities of organic matter seems to be of some value in stopping their spread.

✔ **Powdery mildew:** Plants infected with powdery mildew look as though they've been dusted with talcum powder. This disease requires heat and a brief period of high humidity to form; the attack often occurs after the flowers have finished blooming. Some perennials are highly susceptible to powdery mildew, so plant resistant varieties. If it strikes, cut the stems down to within a few inches of the ground and discard the trimmings. See Figure 12-8.

✔ **Rust:** This disease is so named because it resembles rust on metal. Yellow, orange, or brown bumps that appear on stems or leaves may be caused by rust fungi. Keep plant foliage dry and pick out infected leaves. See Figure 12-9.

✔ **Viruses:** Leaves infected by viruses may be mottled in irregular or sometimes circular patterns or may be yellowed overall. Plant viruses are transmitted by insects. Destroy infected plants and practice good sanitation (wash hands and tools thoroughly).

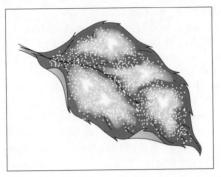

Figure 12-8: Powdery mildew causes leaves to curl and shrivel.

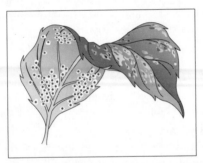

Figure 12-9: Aptly-named rust disease looks like spots of iron rust

✔ **Wilts:** When the whole plant wilts and dies, sometimes overnight, fungal or bacterial root rots may be responsible. Nematodes (described earlier in this list) or gophers can cause the same symptoms. If root rots are the cause, continually wet soil encourages their growth. Improve the drainage and don't replant the same flower in affected soil. If wilt-resistant or wilt-tolerant varieties of your favorite plants are available, plant those instead.

Other Garden Nuisances

Bugs and diseases are not the only pests interested in eating your flowers. King-sized pests can damage more than a few leaves.

Snails and slugs

If large patches of foliage disappear overnight, suspect snails and slugs. These heavy feeders come out at night, so it isn't always obvious who's causing the mischief. Look for telltale silvery slime trails or go outside with a flashlight after dark. You can often find the guilty parties in action.

I get a great deal of satisfaction from taking a pair of scissors into the garden with me at first light and chopping up every slug I can find. The more squeamish among you may prefer to trap the slugs. Moisten a newspaper and roll it loosely into a cylinder. Slugs and snails will seek shelter in it during the daylight hours. You can pick up the paper and dispose of it, sleeping guests and all. Or place a board in the garden — the slugs and snails will seek refuge underneath, and you can easily pick them off.

Wildlife vandals

Deer are undoubtedly the number-one nuisance for suburban gardeners. But the little vole, rabbit, squirrel, or gopher can be just as aggravating. Several options are available for declaring your flowers off-limits to the local wildlife:

- **Physical barriers:** Electric fences discourage deer. Buried hardware cloth — a type of heavy-duty metal mesh sold at building supply stores — prevents burrowing animals from entering the garden underground. Where all else fails, build raised beds and line them with hardware cloth.

- **Repellents:** Repellents are supposed to offend the animal's taste or smell enough to drive it away. The effectiveness of repellents varies. Some animals actually seem to develop a fondness for noxious substances. If you want to give repellents a try, you can buy them at garden centers.

- **Trapping:** Live traps are available to capture small animals. After you catch the little critters, you can release them in an unpopulated area. Be sure to check the trap daily so that the little fellers don't have to go without water for very long.

If animal pests are more than just passing problems, you have two options: Learn to live with them (perhaps by gradually switching over to plants that the pests don't like to eat), or enclose your garden. Enclosing the garden may mean building a fence around it, but draping netting over plants is often effective enough.

Weed Whacking

Contemporary writers struggle over the definition of weed. In the flower garden, no such philosophical introspection is necessary — a *weed* is simply any plant growing where you don't want it to be. This name applies regardless of whether you're referring to an errant plant that's globally accepted as a pest (such as a dandelion) or a Shasta daisy baby boom. If you want three Shasta daisies, the fourth one is a weed — plain and simple.

Besides being misplaced or unattractive, weeds are also bothersome because they're usually much more vigorous plants than your average garden perennial, so they steal water and nutrients from your flowers. Like rude guests who shove their way to be first at the buffet table, the weeds gobble up an unfair share of the water and fertilizer. Weeds may also carry diseases and attract harmful insects.

Weeds come in two main groups — annuals and perennials, just like flowers:

- The annuals form staggering quantities of seed; some produce up to 500,000 per plant. Each of these seeds has the potential to grow into a new weed. The way to stop annuals is to pull them out of your garden before they form seed or to thickly mulch your flower bed so that new weeds can't get sun.

- Perennial weeds are harder to control. They seem to live forever and expand by sending out roots or running stems for several feet in every direction. These weeds want to conquer the world. Pulling and digging at them appears to make them mad; they seem to spread even faster in response. Bindweed is one of the most notorious.

Perennial weeds also form seeds, so don't ever let them get to this stage. Unfortunately, mulch doesn't stop their roots or runners. If you pull out every sprout, you can eventually starve the roots and kill the plant. But if you forget even once, the weed is off and running with renewed enthusiasm.

The most effective way to dispatch perennial weeds is with an herbicide. The safest products are those containing glyphosate. Use the herbicide to kill off all weeds before preparing the soil. Really finishing off persistent types may take several applications. Follow the instructions carefully and remember that these products kill any vegetation, including shrubs and trees. Be certain to confine the spray to the weeds.

Killing perennial weeds in the crowded flower bed

When perennial weeds pop up in an established flower border, getting the herbicide on the weed but not the flowers is difficult. I use a plastic bag to isolate the weed. Here's how:

1. **Cut a hole in the bottom of a plastic bag large enough to fit the weed through.**

2. **Pull the entire weed through the hole in the bottom of the bag.**

3. **Place a stone in the bottom of the bag to hold it in place.**

4. **Carefully spray herbicide into the top of the bag.**

   If you accidentally spray or spill some herbicide on adjoining flowers, immediately rinse them off with water.

5. **Seal the top of the bag with a twist-tie and leave the bag in place until the weed is dead.**

Some perennial flowers are quite weedlike themselves, producing huge amounts of viable seed and scattering it throughout the flower bed. Where you had a trio of flowers a couple of years ago, you now have a large marching band. To prevent this spread, deadhead your flowers. Pull all the seedling plants just as you pull any other weeds.

Pulling weeds

If your soil is loose and crumbly, a light tug is probably all you need to yank out the most stubborn weed. But in dense soil, what usually happens is that you tug at the weed and the top comes off neatly in your hand. The roots happily grow a new top, and the next time you look, the weed is back, looking refreshed and smug!

To kill most weeds, you must get the root. Here's the simplest technique to do so:

1. **Slip the blade of your hand trowel into the ground straight down, next to the main root of the weed.**

2. **Push the trowel blade firmly against the root to loosen it.**

3. **Grab hold of the base of the leaves and pull.**

   Most of the time, this action gets you the whole weed — roots and all.

Chapter 13

Ten Myths about Perennials

*T*his chapter reveals a few rumors and misconceptions for you to be wary of. Disregard these bits of wisdom, no matter who you hear them from. Some get your expectations up too high; others make you do unnecessary work.

Perennial Flowers Live Forever

A few perennials, such as peonies, do live a very long time. Others — blue flax, for example — are as fleeting as annuals. Most perennial flowers manage to hang around for three to seven years. Giving each perennial appropriate cultural conditions and care, of course, has much to do with extending its longevity. Perennials are living plants, after all, and they can be killed by all manner of mistakes.

Perennials Are Less Work Than Annuals

The assumption that perennials are easier to manage than annuals arises from the fact that, unlike annuals, perennials grow back year after year. However, each year, some perennials die and have to be replaced. No garden is labor-free, not even a garden of perennials, so grow perennials because you like to work in the garden, not because you're trying to impress your mother-in-law or your neighbors.

A Perfect Garden Climate Exists Somewhere

If this myth were true, all the serious gardeners would have discovered this paradise and moved there long ago. Human nature being what it is, they wouldn't be able to keep the climate's location a secret because they would boast about it. Garden magazine articles and books would talk about this place, and you'd know where it is, too. All gardeners, no matter where they live, have to cope with bad weather, pests (large and small), and the frustrations of not being able to grow some plant that they have their hearts set on.

Native Perennials Are Easier to Grow

This one occasionally pops up in books and articles about native plants. The idea is based on the fact that flowers from the field or the roadside care for themselves. After all, no one is tending them in the wild. This theory is true in some cases but not all, depending entirely on which flower you're trying to tame.

One of the most widespread families of wildflowers in the western U.S. — the paintbrushes (*Castilleja*) — are nearly impossible to grow in a garden. Some folks manage to keep a few alive, but I've never seen the masses that are so common in nature duplicated in anyone's garden. Wildflowers can be very fussy and exacting in their requirements. Garden flowers, on the other hand, have often been subjected to decades of selective breeding that eliminated the persnickety among them ages ago.

Growing Flowers in the Shade Is Impossible

Growing sun-loving flowers in the shaded garden is impossible. The trick to successful shade gardening is to select flowers that prefer shade. Fortunately, you have dozens of shade-lovers to choose from, so you have no excuse not to have just as successful a flower garden in the shadows as in the sun. Check out Chapter 5 for lists of shade-lovers and tips to keep your shady characters happy.

Nature Always Arranges Flowers in Groups

Where wildflowers can spread out casually into colonies, they often do so. But nature isn't that predictable. Fields of wildflowers are sometimes a real mixture, with placement as random as a tossed salad. If you prefer your flowers in groups, by all means arrange them that way. If you like them all mixed up, that's okay, too.

Purple Coneflowers Are Drought Tolerant

Purple coneflowers have developed a reputation for drought tolerance because they can survive a dry season several months long when they're grown in damp climates. But many people mistakenly apply this fact to drier regions. Now purple coneflowers show up on every xeriscape (dry-climate gardening) list.

Drought tolerance is a relative term. Purple coneflowers are not happy campers in arid and semiarid regions. They can endure rainless spells, but the rest of the year they want water — a lot of water. I don't mean to pick on purple coneflowers; I just want to warn you to exercise healthy skepticism whenever you come across gardening advice that doesn't measure up with your own experiences or the experiences of other gardeners in your region.

You Have to Cut Iris Fans After They Bloom

Your grandmother may insist that you cut iris leaves into triangular configurations after the flowers fade, but this activity just creates busy work for you — and it isn't very good for the iris, either. Plants feed themselves through their leaves. When you cut down the amount of surface space they have to catch sunlight, you put your iris on a diet. Just cut the dead flower stalks so that the plant doesn't waste energy forming seed and then pull off browned foliage — all year round — to keep your irises clean and healthy.

Always Clean Up the Flower Bed in the Fall

You can clean up the flower bed if you want, but if you're really busy in the fall, you can also wait until spring to do the major housekeeping. Do make time in the fall to remove diseased leaves and replace the mulch under any of your plants that were plagued by insects during the growing season to prevent eggs and larvae from spending the winter there, all tucked up and cozy in the mulch. But leave the rest of the debris in place to create a natural winter mulch to protect the crown of the plants during winter's coldest weather.

Orange and Pink Clash

Mothers and garden designers perpetuate this myth, but clashing colors aren't covered in natural laws. You know what you like, so don't be intimidated into limiting yourself to other people's color tastes. Orange and pink flowers sometimes look stunning together. Everyone's favorite, purple coneflower, is a daisy with pink rays surrounding orange centers.

Index

BUSINESS, CAREERS & PERSONAL FINANCE

0-7645-9847-3

0-7645-2431-3

Also available:
- Business Plans Kit For Dummies
  0-7645-9794-9
- Economics For Dummies
  0-7645-5726-2
- Grant Writing For Dummies
  0-7645-8416-2
- Home Buying For Dummies
  0-7645-5331-3
- Managing For Dummies
  0-7645-1771-6
- Marketing For Dummies
  0-7645-5600-2
- Personal Finance For Dummies
  0-7645-2590-5*

- Resumes For Dummies
  0-7645-5471-9
- Selling For Dummies
  0-7645-5363-1
- Six Sigma For Dummies
  0-7645-6798-5
- Small Business Kit For Dummies
  0-7645-5984-2
- Starting an eBay Business For Dummies
  0-7645-6924-4
- Your Dream Career For Dummies
  0-7645-9795-7

HOME & BUSINESS COMPUTER BASICS

0-7645-8958-X

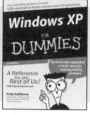

0-7645-7326-8

Also available:
- Buying a Computer For Dummies
  0-7645-9818-X
- Cleaning Windows XP For Dummies
  0-7645-7549-X
- Excel 2003 All-in-One Desk Reference For Dummies
  0-7645-3758-X
- Excel Formulas and Functions For Dummies
  0-7645-7556-2
- Mac OS X Tiger For Dummies
  0-7645-7675-5

- Office 2003 All-in-One Desk Reference For Dummies
  0-7645-3883-7
- QuickBooks All-in-One Desk Reference For Dummies
  0-7645-7662-3
- Quicken 2006 For Dummies
  0-7645-9658-6
- RFID For Dummies
  0-7645-7910-X
- Salesforce.com For Dummies
  0-7645-7921-5
- Upgrading and Fixing Laptops For Dummies
  0-7645-8959-8
- Word 2003 For Dummies
  0-7645-3982-5

FOOD, HOME, GARDEN, HOBBIES, MUSIC & PETS

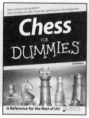

0-7645-8404-9

0-7645-9904-6

Also available:
- Candy Making For Dummies
  0-7645-9734-5
- Card Games For Dummies
  0-7645-9910-0
- Crocheting For Dummies
  0-7645-4151-X
- Dog Training For Dummies
  0-7645-8418-9
- Healthy Carb Cookbook For Dummies
  0-7645-8476-6
- Home Maintenance For Dummies
  0-7645-5215-5

- Horses For Dummies
  0-7645-9797-3
- Jewelry Making & Beading For Dummies
  0-7645-2571-9
- Orchids For Dummies
  0-7645-6759-4
- Puppies For Dummies
  0-7645-5255-4
- Rock Guitar For Dummies
  0-7645-5356-9
- Sewing For Dummies
  0-7645-6847-7
- Singing For Dummies
  0-7645-2475-5

INTERNET & DIGITAL MEDIA

0-7645-9802-3

0-7645-5654-1

Also available:
- BitTorrent For Dummies
  0-7645-9981-X
- Blogging For Dummies
  0-471-77084-1
- Digital SLR Cameras and Photography For Dummies
  0-7645-9803-1
- Digital Video For Dummies
  0-471-78278-5
- Firefox For Dummies
  0-471-74899-4
- Home Recording For Musicians
  0-7645-8884-2

- iPods & iTunes For Dummies
  0-471-74739-4
- Google Search & Rescue For Dummies
  0-7645-9930-5
- The Internet For Dummies
  0-7645-8996-2
- Podcasting For Dummies
  0-471-74898-6
- Search Engine Optimization For Dummies
  0-7645-6758-6
- VoIP For Dummies
  0-7645-8843-5

SPORTS, FITNESS, PARENTING, RELIGION & SPIRITUALITY

0-471-76871-5   0-7645-7841-3

Also available:
- Catholicism For Dummies
  0-7645-5391-7
- Exercise Balls For Dummies
  0-7645-5623-1
- Fitness For Dummies
  0-7645-7851-0
- Football For Dummies
  0-7645-3936-1
- Judaism For Dummies
  0-7645-5299-6
- Potty Training For Dummies
  0-7645-5417-4
- Buddhism For Dummies
  0-7645-5359-3

- Pregnancy For Dummies
  0-7645-4483-7 †
- Ten Minute Tone-Ups
  For Dummies
  0-7645-7207-5
- NASCAR For Dummies
  0-7645-7681-X
- Religion For Dummies
  0-7645-5264-3
- Soccer For Dummies
  0-7645-5229-5
- Women in the Bible
  For Dummies
  0-7645-8475-8

TRAVEL

0-7645-7749-2   0-7645-6945-7

Also available:
- Alaska For Dummies
  0-7645-7746-8
- Cruise Vacations For Dummies
  0-7645-6941-4
- England For Dummies
  0-7645-4276-1
- Europe For Dummies
  0-7645-7529-5
- Germany For Dummies
  0-7645-7823-5
- Hawaii For Dummies
  0-7645-7402-7

- Italy For Dummies
  0-7645-7386-1
- Las Vegas For Dummies
  0-7645-7382-9
- London For Dummies
  0-7645-4277-X
- Paris For Dummies
  0-7645-7630-5
- RV Vacations For Dummies
  0-7645-4442-X
- Walt Disney World & Orlando
  For Dummies
  0-7645-9660-8

GRAPHICS, DESIGN & WEB DEVELOPMENT

0-7645-8815-X   0-7645-9571-7

Also available:
- 3D Game Animation For
  Dummies
  0-7645-8789-7
- AutoCAD 2006 For Dummies
  0-7645-8925-3
- Building a Web Site For
  Dummies
  0-7645-7144-3
- Creating Web Pages All-in-
  One Desk Reference For
  Dummies
  0-7645-4345-8
- Dreamweaver 8 For Dummies
  0-7645-9649-7
- InDesign CS2 For Dummies
  0-7645-9572-5

- Macromedia Flash 8
  For Dummies
  0-7645-9691-8
- Photoshop CS2 and Digital
  Photography For Dummies
  0-7645-9580-6
- Photoshop Elements 4
  For Dummies
  0-471-77483-9
- Syndicating Web Sites with
  RSS Feeds For Dummies
  0-7645-8848-6
- Yahoo! SiteBuilder
  For Dummies
  0-7645-9800-7

NETWORKING, SECURITY, PROGRAMMING & DATABASES

0-7645-7728-X   0-471-74940-0

Also available:
- Access 2003 All-in-One Desk
  Reference For Dummies
  0-7645-3988-4
- ASP.NET 2 For Dummies
  0-7645-7907-X
- C# 2005 For Dummies
  0-7645-9704-3
- Excel VBA Programming
  For Dummies
  0-7645-7412-4
- Hacking For Dummies
  0-7645-5784-X
- Hacking Wireless Networks
  For Dummies
  0-7645-9730-2

- Microsoft SQL Server 2005
  For Dummies
  0-7645-7755-7
- Networking All-in-One Desk
  Reference For Dummies
  0-7645-9939-9
- Preventing Identity Theft
  For Dummies
  0-7645-7336-5
- Telecom For Dummies
  0-471-77085-X
- Visual Studio 2005 All-in-One
  Desk Reference For Dummies
  0-7645-9775-2
- XML For Dummies
  0-7645-8845-1

HEALTH & SELF-HELP

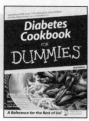

0-7645-8450-2   0-7645-4149-8

Also available:

- Bipolar Disorder For Dummies
  0-7645-8451-0
- Chemotherapy and Radiation For Dummies
  0-7645-7832-4
- Controlling Cholesterol For Dummies
  0-7645-5440-9
- Diabetes For Dummies
  0-7645-6820-5* †
- Divorce For Dummies
  0-7645-8417-0 †
- Fibromyalgia For Dummies
  0-7645-5441-7

- Low-Calorie Dieting For Dummies
  0-7645-9905-4
- Meditation For Dummies
  0-471-77774-9
- Osteoporosis For Dummies
  0-7645-7621-6
- Overcoming Anxiety For Dummies
  0-7645-5447-6
- Reiki For Dummies
  0-7645-9907-0
- Stress Management For Dummies
  0-7645-5144-2

EDUCATION, HISTORY, REFERENCE & TEST PREPARATION

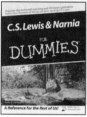

0-7645-8381-6   0-7645-9554-7

Also available:

- The ACT For Dummies
  0-7645-9652-7
- Algebra For Dummies
  0-7645-5325-9
- Algebra Workbook For Dummies
  0-7645-8467-7
- Astronomy For Dummies
  0-7645-8465-0
- Calculus For Dummies
  0-7645-2498-4
- Chemistry For Dummies
  0-7645-5430-1
- Forensics For Dummies
  0-7645-5580-4

- Freemasons For Dummies
  0-7645-9796-5
- French For Dummies
  0-7645-5193-0
- Geometry For Dummies
  0-7645-5324-0
- Organic Chemistry I For Dummies
  0-7645-6902-3
- The SAT I For Dummies
  0-7645-7193-1
- Spanish For Dummies
  0-7645-5194-9
- Statistics For Dummies
  0-7645-5423-9

Get smart @ dummies.com®

- **Find a full list of Dummies titles**
- **Look into loads of FREE on-site articles**
- **Sign up for FREE eTips e-mailed to you weekly**
- **See what other products carry the Dummies name**
- **Shop directly from the Dummies bookstore**
- **Enter to win new prizes every month!**

---

* **Separate Canadian edition also available**
† **Separate U.K. edition also available**

Portable Gardening Guides

**Each book includes
8 pages of full-color
garden photos!**

Notes